A Century and a Half of Delta Kappa Epsilon

The Illustrated History of Delta Kappa Epsilon

Edited by: Duncan Andrews (Rho, 1957)
Past Chairman of the Fraternity

A Century and a Half of DKE
The Illustrated History of Delta Kappa Epsilon

Edited by Duncan Andrews (Rho, 1957)

Published by:
Heritage Publishers, Inc.
1536 E. Maryland Ave.
Phoenix, Arizona 85014-1448
(602) 277-4780, (800) 972-8507
for Rampant Lion Foundation
Grosse Pointe Farms, Michigan

ISBN 0-929690-33-8
Library of Congress Catalog Number 97-70228

Printed and bound in the United States of America

GERALD R. FORD

To My Brothers in DKE:

It is a great pleasure and honor to have the opportunity to write this preface to the long awaited 150 Year History of Delta Kappa Epsilon.

I prize my experiences at the Deke house in Ann Arbor, and on the University of Michigan campus. The friendships I made there and later with Delta Kappa Epsilon Brothers from around the continent have served me well.

It is no coincidence that four Presidents of the United States have been Dekes and that our flag was flown with the Stars and Stripes on the first expedition to the North Pole, and flew on a manned landing on the moon. The individual qualities that DKE seeks have certainly withstood the test of time and served us all in good stead. It is that unique blend of leadership, brotherhood and tradition that fuels this Fraternity.

I particularly want to thank benefactors William E. Simon, C. Allen Favrot and all of the sponsors for their help in getting this work to press. Finally, I want to take this opportunity to extend my warmest, best wishes to all present, past and future Dekes and their families.

Gerald R. Ford
Omicron "35"

BENEFACTORS & SPONSORS

BENEFACTORS

William E. Simon, Rho '53
C. Allen Favrot, Tau Lambda '47

SPONSORS

Louis F. Bantle, Phi Gamma '51
George H. Bass, Theta '37
W. Streeter Bass, Theta '38
James D. Bishop, Phi '56
Lyman G. Bloomingdale, Upsilon '35
James M. Broomas, Omega Chi '76
Charles S. Brown, Jr., Phi Gamma '86
Robert H. Brown, Jr., Sigma Tau '54
Thomas W. Chalfont, Mu '53
Winfield C. Chapin Foundation
David C. Clapp, Phi '60
Angus R. Cooper,II, Psi '64
Hugh F. Culverhouse, Psi '41
Robert L. Davis, III, Beta '42
William E. DesJardins, Omicron '50
James A. Diamond, Zeta '89
Frederick H. Dohmen, Rho Delta '39
Peter A. Dow, Omicron '55
B. D. Drayton, Jr., Alpha Chi '57
David K. Easlick, Jr., Omicron '69
H. Chotard Eustis, III, Tau Lambda '68
Bruce F. Evans, Kappa Epsilon '40
Clifford F. Favrot, Jr., Tau Lambda '44
Calvin C. Fearon, Phi Gamma '60
Donald G. Fisher, Theta Zeta '51
Gerald R. Ford, Omicron '35
William N. Garbarini, Phi Gamma '62
E. Freeman Gossett, Theta Rho '43
William W. Gresham, Jr., Tau Lambda '47
James M. Hacker, Omicron '69
Samuel F. Heffner, Jr., Psi Omega '56
John W. Holman, Jr., Upsilon '59
Herbert D. Kelleher, Gamma Phi '53
Thomas B. Ketchum, Phi '72
Allan P. Kirby, Jr., Rho'53
John W. Lambrecht, Omicron '67
Peter K. Leisure, Phi '52
Charles H. Lloyd, Sigma Alpha '72
Reuben Mark, Alpha Alpha '60
Conrad H. McEachern, Jr., Zeta Zeta '56
James McKee, Jr., Phi Gamma '40
M. Stanford McMillan, Gamma '89
Donald G. McNeely, Phi '37
B. Milo Mitchell, Delta Kappa '25
Charles D. Mitchell, Phi '34
Mu of DKE Foundation
Edmond A. Neal, Sr., Upsilon '36
George A. Nicholson, Jr., Omicron '28
Robert W. Olson, Theta '63
Douglas B. Padnos, Omicron '77
C. Wrede Petersmeyer, Theta Zeta '41
Paul D. Pitzer, Gamma '75
Rho Delta Alumni Association
John G. Robinson, Mu '60
William B. Ruger, Beta '40
Arthur C. Settlage, Theta Zeta '33
Andrew J. Shoup, Jr., Zeta Zeta '57
Fred H. Sills, Delta Delta '33
Stephen H. Smith, Tau Delta '76
Phineas Sprague, Theta '50
John H. Stembler, Jr., Beta '65
Richard C. Stoker, Beta '60
Walter J. Vollrath, Jr. Rho Delta '39
Donald A. Weadon, Jr., Delta Chi '67
John R. Wilson, Mu '52
John W. Wirtz, Omicron '47
William Wrigley, Phi '54
George H. Zinn, Jr., Omicron '55

The Chapters of DKE International Fraternity

Date of Founding	Chapter [Inactive]
June 22, 1844	Phi...Yale University, New Haven, CT
November 5, 1844	Theta...Bowdoin College, Brunswick, ME
September 15, 1845	Zeta...Princeton University, Princeton, NJ
June 25, 1846	Xi...Colby College, Waterville, ME
November 1, 1846	Sigma...Amherst College, Amherst, MA
April 19, 1847	Gamma...Vanderbilt University, Nashville, TN
June 20, 1847	Psi...University of Alabama, Tuscaloosa, AL
April 14, 1850	Chi...University of Mississippi, Oxford, MS [1985]
July 25, 1850	Upsilon...Brown University, Providence, RI
April 4, 1851	Beta...University of North Carolina, Chapel Hill, NC
October 15, 1851	Alpha...Harvard University, Cambridge, MA
March 8, 1852	Kappa...Miami University, Oxford, OH
May 5, 1852	Delta...South Carolina College, Columbia, SC [1861]
June 5, 1852	Lambda...Kenyon College, Gambier, OH
September, 1852	Omega...University of Oakland, Oakland, MS [1861]
November 26, 1852	Eta...University of Virginia, Charlottesville, VA
July 14, 1853	Pi...Dartmouth College, Hanover, NH [1970]
February 1854	Iota...Centre College, Danville, KY
September 19, 1854	Alpha Alpha...Middlebury College, Middlebury, VT
February 24, 1855	Omicron...University of Michigan, Ann Arbor, MI
March 25, 1855	Epsilon...Williams College, Williamstown, MA [1961]
October 15, 1855	Rho...Lafayette College, Easton, PA
January 15, 1856	Tau...Hamilton College, Clinton, NY
March 1, 1856	Mu...Colgate University, Hamilton, NY
August 1, 1856	Nu...C.C.N.Y., New York, NY [1973]
November 1, 1856	Beta Phi...University of Rochester, Rochester, NY
November 25, 1856	Theta Chi...Union University, Schenectady, NY [1869]
March 16, 1857	Kappa Psi...Cumberland University, Lebanon, TN [1874]
January 30, 1858	Zeta Zeta...Louisiana State University, Baton Rouge, LA
June 10, 1858	Alpha Delta...Jefferson College, Canonsburg, PA [1862]
February 1861	[1st] Tau Delta...Union University, Murfreesboro, TN[1865]
February 14, 1861	Phi Chi...Rutgers University, New Brunswick, NJ
May 1861	Kappa Phi...Troy University, Troy, NY [1865]
November 8, 1866	Psi Phi...Depauw University, Greencastle, IN
January 18, 1867	Gamma Phi...Wesleyan University, Middletown, CT
June 4, 1867	Eta Alpha...Washington & Lee University, Lexington, VA [1871]
November 14, 1867	Psi Omega...Rensselaer Poly. Institute, Troy, NY
November 17, 1868	Beta Chi...Case Western Reserve, Cleveland, OH
February 11, 1870	Delta Chi...Cornell University, Ithaca, NY
May 22, 1879	Delta Delta...University of Chicago, Chicago, IL
November 17, 1871	Phi Gamma...Syracuse University, Syracuse, NY
October 15, 1874	Gamma Beta...Columbia University, New York, NY [1935]

THE CHAPTERS OF DKE INTERNATIONAL FRATERNITY

DATE OF FOUNDING	CHAPTER [INACTIVE]
December 8, 1876	Theta Zeta...University of Calif. at Berkeley, Berkeley, CA
May 5, 1879	Alpha Chi...Trinity College, Hartford, CT [1990]
October 16, 1889	Phi Epsilon... University of Minnesota, Minneapolis, MN
November 14, 1890	Sigma Tau...Massachusetts Inst. of Tech., Boston, MA
November 17, 1898	Tau Lambda... Tulane University, New Orleans, LA
November 17, 1897	Alpha Phi...University of Toronto, Toronto, ONT
November 16, 1899	Delta Kappa...University of Pennsylvania, Philadelphia, PA
November 15, 1900	Tau Alpha... McGill University, Montreal, QUE [1989]
December 12, 1901	Sigma Rho...Stanford University, Stanford, CA
November 17, 1904	Delta Pi...University of Illinois, Champaign, IL [1986]
November 15, 1906	Rho Delta...University of Wisconsin, Madison, WI
November 18, 1910	Kappa Epsilon...University of Washington, Seattle, WA
December 6, 1912	Omega Chi...University of Texas, Austin, TX
March 27, 1925	Alpha Tau...University of Manitoba, Winnepeg, MAN
February 13, 1932	Theta Rho...UCLA, Los Angeles, CA
December 30, 1932	Delta Phi...University of Alberta, Edmonton, ALTA
February 27, 1948	Delta Epsilon...Northwestern University, Evanston, IL [1959]
March 27, 1949	Lambda Delta...Southern Methodist University, Dallas, TX [1961]
February 26, 1949	Phi Alpha...University of British Columbia, Vancouver, BC
February 16, 1952	Kappa Delta...University of Maryland, College Park, MD
February 21, 1954	University of Oklahoma, Norman, OK [1995]
February 22, 1969	[2nd] Tau Delta...University of the South, Sewanee, TN
March 18, 1970	Psi Delta...Wake Forest University, Winston-Salem, NC
February 6, 1971	Sigma Alpha...Virginia Poly. Inst., Blacksburg, VA
June 1, 1972	Phi Delta...University of Western Ontario, London, ONT
January 23, 1973	Sigma Phi...Villanova University, Bryn Mawr, PA [1993]
April 8, 1976	Pi Beta...Troy State University, Troy, AL [1986]
May 4, 1982	Alpha Mu...Rowan College, Glassboro, NJ
April 17, 1983	Epsilon Rho...Duke University, Durham, NC
April 24, 1983	Nu Zeta...Pace University, Pleasantville, NY
May 19, 1984	Alpha Omega...Louisiana Technical University, Ruston, LA
April 13, 1985	Theta Upsilon...Arizona State University, Tempe, AZ
December 8, 1990	Iota Mu...Fordham University, New York, NY
December 8, 1990	Alpha Rho...Temple University, Philadelphia, PA [1995]
January 12, 1991	Zeta Upsilon...University of California at Davis, Davis, CA
January 26, 1991	Phi Sigma...Bryant College, Smithfield, RI
February 16, 1991	Phi Rho...Penn State University, State College, PA
February 16, 1991	Chi Rho...Bloomsburg University, Bloomsburg, PA
April 27, 1991	Zeta Chi...Bentley College, Waltham, MA
June 26, 1993	Omega Omega...University of Arizona, Tucson, AZ [1995]
June 26, 1993	Sigma Beta...University of California, Santa Barbara, CA
June 12, 1994	Gamma Beta...New York University, New York, NY
February 25, 1995	Beta Delta...University of Georgia, Athens, GA

CONTENTS

INTRODUCTION

WHAT IS DELTA KAPPA EPSILON?

The fraternity gives its members a home and congenial associates when he enters college; it sets before him noble ideals of manhood and high incentives which help draw out the best that is in him, it spurs him on to excel in scholarship and other branches of undergraduate activity; it sets a guard over his conduct lest he bring reproach upon the pin he wears with so much pride; in the management of its affairs, it gives him a practical business training; in its halls he gets a drill on debating and speaking which proves a lasting benefit; its chapter house becomes almost a home for him, with all the influence of good which this implies; its intercollegiate feature broadens his view of the educational world and renders doubly pleasant his visits to sister colleges and his meetings with college men all through life; it gives him as an undergraduate the benefits of the acquaintance of many alumni, a circumstance which becomes a valuable asset when he enters upon his life-work; and it gives him precious friendships which will be cherished among his dearest possessions while life remains.

John Clair Minot (Theta, 1896)
Past Honorary President of DKE

Defining the Brotherhood

"To me DKE was head and shoulders over any other house on campus."

Anonymous

Delta Kappa Epsilon has always been an organization dedicated to helping Brothers, commonly referred to as "Dekes," become leaders. Within its bonds, young men learn the value of personal development as they strive to build skills in interpersonal relationships and teamwork, and learn to appreciate others for their differences.

The Fraternity has always attracted young men of quality, offering them more than just a social circle or academic society. In the *DKE Handbook for Pledges*, an anonymous Deke described his first impression of DKE when he entered college:

> To me DKE was head and shoulders over any other house on campus. I do not hold to an opinion without factual evidence. Apart from DKE's leadership in collegiate activity (which honor may be shared) there is the peculiar status of this fraternity on whatever campus, which depends not on college activity nor even on personnel. It commands respect, however reluctant, of all rivals—an abstract "something-about-it" peculiarity which sets DKE above and beyond other orders undeniably in a class by itself.
>
> This strange, revered quality remained a mystic secret beyond comprehension until formal initiation began. Its characteristics are seen in Dekes wherever met—strength of character, manliness, an air of self-respect, decency, and a degree of sophistication in the true sense of culture.

The foundation of DKE is its Ritual, which W. Hubert Beal (Delta Pi, 1916) described as "a prayer for the right life and the good life of one and all." The founders were deeply religious men who did not separate their faith from their everyday lives, and in so doing, strove to live their lives according to the laws of God. The Ritual bespeaks these high standards through brotherhood and tradition, teaching Dekes to be wise, strong, courageous, kind, and honorable.

The oldest international secret fraternity of New England origin, DKE has Brothers in every profession, and its rolls contain the names of many famous and influential men. The roster of leaders who are Brothers runs the gamut: foreign ambassadors, judges, state chief justices, congressmen, governors, cabinet members, sports figures, university presidents and deans, entertainment stars, generals, religious leaders, educators, attorneys, physicians, bankers, writers, publishers, scientists, chief executive officers, and world renowned explorers, among others, U.S. Presidents Rutherford B. Hayes (Delta Chi, Hon.), Theodore Roosevelt (Alpha, 1880), Gerald R. Ford (Omicron, 1935), and George H. W. Bush (Phi, 1948) may have had differing philosophies for the country's success, but all shared the Brotherhood of Delta Kappa Epsilon.

Whether DKE shapes its members for success or attracts men destined for greatness is a question that may never be answered. However, the Brotherhood has always called for certain qualities in its members. These include financial and personal integrity, a sense of obligation and responsibility, and a high standard of scholarship. The Fraternity believes these qualities are essential to the development and growth of a leaders, as is "an active and energetic character."

"It has always been a very select fraternity," recalled Past President Charles Blaisdell (Pi, 1937). "Everyone who became a pledge and then a member was of solid scholastic standing and was well rounded. They were active in athletics and the performing arts."

"Americans...constantly form associations."

Alexis de Tocqueville

Brotherhood and good fellowship characterized the fraternity through its first 150 years. As Dr. Edward Griffin Bartlett (Phi, 1844), a DKE founder, described it:

> We built better than we knew, when we founded the brotherhood to which good-fellowship has ever been a passport not less requisite than learning. Where glees have been written as often as essays, and where the candidate most favored was he who combined in the most equal of proportions the gentleman, the scholar, and the jolly good fellow.

The Birth of the American Fraternity

DKE's success cannot be completely appreciated without an understanding of its history as well as the birth of fraternities in general.

Alexis de Tocqueville, a French traveler and historian, once wrote, "Americans . . . constantly form associations. They are the most fraternal people in the world." Indeed, fraternities are uniquely American. Of course, there were various kinds of student organizations on the European continent, but none

It was not until 1776 that the grandfather of modern fraternities came into being...

broke the bounds of individual colleges and universities; they were strictly local.

Early American universities closely resembled their European models. The academic focus was on Greek and Latin languages and biblical studies. Students spent long, arduous hours disciplining their minds and polishing their oratorical skills. Their behavior and dress were strictly monitored, and few social distractions were offered to help the young men develop character and charm. The independent thinking that has always been characteristic of the American spirit, however, could not be quenched, and things gradually changed.

The fraternity movement began around 1750 at the College of William and Mary in Williamsburg, Virginia, with the formation of an undergraduate social group, known as the Flat Hat Club, which congregated for merriment and to discuss the issues of the day. By 1772 the group was defunct, replaced by literary societies and oratorical clubs.

It was not until 1776 that the grandfather of modern fraternities came into being, again at the College of William and Mary, after a blameless scholar of Greek, John Heath, was rejected by one of the student organizations. Heath and four friends thereupon founded their own group which they called Phi Beta Kappa. At that meeting, of December 5, 1776, five months after the signing of the Declaration of Independence, the fledgling society adopted a secret oath, motto, ritual, and pin or "badge." Although the three stars on the medallion stood for fraternity, morality, and literature, the faculty opposed the organization because they believed it would undermine their influence over students. Their resistance, however, could not squelch the enthusiasm of the newfound brothers, and Phi Beta Kappa established a chapter at Yale in 1780, followed by one at Harvard the next year.

By the early nineteenth century, the nation was experiencing unprecedented changes in thought and practices. On the political front, aristocracy was giving way to democracy. Moral issues such as slavery and abolition were drawing increasingly heated debate. Women yearned for rights of their own, and choices in religious affiliation grew.

In a time of such upheaval, it is little wonder that young men found secret societies appealing. Fraternities grew at an astonishing rate, despite the expanding anti-secret society sentiment from college faculty, church officials, and others who believed the secrecy concealed immorality and debauchery. Some went so far as to say it was impossible to be a Christian and a fraternity member at the same time.

Yet Greek letter fraternities grew as young men were drawn to colleagues of like mind and common interests in bonds of brotherhood and secrecy. The appeal of the forbidden groups was described by Aldice G. Warren (Beta Phi, 1883) in a 1910 history of DKE:

> Founded in almost every instance upon the loftiest ideals; embracing among its members, at least in theory, only the choicest spirits of the colleges in which its chapters are established; knitting them together by bonds of the closest friendship; through the older and graduate members, keeping a watch and ward over the younger ones at once fraternal and paternal; aiding them by counsel and material help, and ever ready to assist them when starting out upon their careers after graduation; giving to its alumni an increased interest in the whole life of the college because of their interest in the chapter; the Greek Letter Fraternity has become one of the most potent factors in the college life of today.

"...the Greek Letter Fraternity has become one of the most potent factors in college life of today."

Aldice G. Warren (Beta Phi, 1883) in a 1910 history of DKE

One of these societies was established in 1812 when four men from Phi Beta Kappa founded the first Kappa Alpha at the University of North Carolina. Several "circles" or chapters formed in the South, but internal dissension eventually led to the fraternity's dismantling.

On November 26, 1825, the Kappa Alpha Society was founded at Union College in Schenectady, New York. Two years later, Sigma Phi and Delta Phi were founded there to compete with KA, forming the Union Triad. Because the president of Union College, Eliphalet Nott, was receptive to student associations, several fraternities were established there, and Union eventually became known as the "Mother of Fraternities."

However, at the same time, radical opposition to the groups gained momentum, fueled by the 1826 kidnapping of William Morgan from Canandaigua, New York. He was preparing to print a book revealing the secrets of the Masonic Order, a non-collegiate secret society that had been influential for many years, with valued citizens on its rolls. Morgan was taken to Niagara Falls and from that point vanished.

Faced with this unfairness, a band of fifteen students set out to establish their own society, and Delta Kappa Epsilon was born.

The Masons adamantly denied involvement in Morgan's disappearance, but the backlash toward secret societies in general was fierce. Universities and colleges adopted laws forbidding students to join fraternities, often expelling discovered members. Phi Beta Kappa, forced to divulge its secrets, became strictly an academic honor society.

A Time of Discontent

A natural rivalry developed between Greek letter fraternities, and each maintained constant communication with its "branches." By the 1840s two such junior class societies had become fixtures at Yale: Alpha Delta Phi, founded at Hamilton College in 1832, and Psi Upsilon, founded at Union College in 1833. Each year the best and the brightest sophomores were elected to one or the other of these fraternities, and it eventually became easy to predict which students would receive such invitations.

In theory the election of members was based on good scholarship and personal character, but in 1844 political maneuvering resulted in elections that appeared to be woefully unfair. Many students who had excelled in academics and were considered men of character were not extended invitations. Dr. Bartlett later recalled, "So marked was the partiality with which the selection had been made, so prominent were the instances in which merit had been slighted, as the event in college honors afterwards showed, that elections were rejected by several who had actually received them."

Faced with this unfairness, a band of fifteen students set out to establish their own society, and Delta Kappa Epsilon was born.

CHAPTER 1
BUILDING A BROTHERHOOD

After the Alpha Delta Phi and Psi Upsilon elections, several men from the class of 1846 suggested starting a new society with less restrictive criteria. No one can say who should be credited for organizing Delta Kappa Epsilon, but the zeal of George Foot Chester had a profound effect on the other interested students and propelled the idea into reality. On Saturday, June 22, 1844, fifteen students gathered in room twelve of Old South Hall to begin a new fraternity based on broader and more democratic principles than had been experienced in such organizations. They adopted the name Delta Kappa Epsilon, devised a secret grip, and formulated the Greek motto: "From the heart, friends forever!" They sketched a design for a pin that depicted the letters "DKE" on a scroll upon a diamond shape with a star in each corner. The word "Yale" was added to the final design.

"Five of DKE's Founders" Dr. Edward G. Bartlett, Hon. William Boyd Jacobs, Col. George Foot Chester, Prof. Edward V. S. Kinsley and Dr. Elisha B. Shapleigh.

Two weeks later a committee chaired by William Walter Horton drew up the written articles that organized the Brotherhood. William Woodruff Atwater, Edward Griffin Bartlett, Frederick Peter Bellinger Jr., Henry Case, George Foot Chester, John Butler Conyngham, Thomas Isaac Franklin, William Walter Horton, William Boyd Jacobs, Edward Van Schoonhoven Kinsley, Chester Newell Righter, Elisha Bacon Shapleigh, Thomas Du Bois Sherwood, Albert Everett Stetson, and Orson William Stow signed the document and thereby became the founding members of DKE.

These men had more in mind for their newborn organization than to become a duplicate of the other two junior societies at Yale. They regarded academic honors highly, but they also looked for other qualities in members. They took into account good company and common tastes and interests, making DKE a true fraternity.

The members held subsequent meetings in a hall on the corner of State and Chapel streets. Oblivious to the lackluster surroundings and shortage of furniture, the new Brothers began polishing their literary and oratoratorical skills. Their efforts paid off when the university announced honors for the class of 1846: all members received recognition for scholarship, and several took honors in various college exercises. Such a strong showing increased the founders' excitement and justified their belief that their academic merits had been overlooked by the other junior societies on the campus. And, in addition, they had the qualities of Brotherhood based on friendship rooted in personal compatibility.

Seeds are Sown

At first the founders had no plans to establish chapters at other colleges, but DKE became an intercollegiate fraternity in the same year it was founded. In correspondence to his boyhood friend John S.H. Fogg at Bowdoin College in Brunswick, Maine, Bacon Shapleigh conveyed such enthusiasm for DKE that Fogg was intrigued. Shapleigh and Bartlett eventually visited Bowdoin and were duly impressed with the caliber of men they met there. Accordingly, Theta Chapter was installed on that campus on November 6, 1844. Members of the new chapter were so enthusiastic that word of DKE soon spread to neighboring Waterville (later named Colby) College and Amherst. At this point the Yale chapter adopted the name Phi and began its role as DKE's head chapter.

Lambda's Log Cabin circa 1854.

New England and the mid-Atlantic states proved fertile ground for the Brotherhood, resulting in charters at Brown University (Upsilon) and Harvard (Alpha) in 1851. Yet interest in DKE was not limited to the northern states. Many wealthy southerners sent their sons to Yale, where they were attracted to the high standards and fellowship of DKE. Aldice Warren described these men in the 1910 *Catalogue of DKE*: "Warm-hearted, enthusiastic, brilliant in oratory and debate, firm in their friendships, skilled in political strategy as well as in scholarship, leaders in every branch of college activity." So many of these young men joined Delta Kappa Epsilon that it became known as the "Southerners' Fraternity." Two DKE founders, Horton and Franklin, were, in fact, from below the Mason-Dixon Line, and from the two following classes, thirteen of thirty-eight Brothers were from the South. DKE was the first Northern fraternity to colonize heavily in the South, establishing chapters at prestigious schools throughout the region. Gamma was chartered at Vanderbilt and Psi at Alabama in 1847, by 1861 a dozen Southern chapters were thriving.

DKE's fast-paced growth was fueled by enthusiasm, loyalty, and determination in the North and by a carefully constructed expansion plan in the South. By the end of its first decade, DKE

Yale Tomb.

had granted twenty charters, seventeen of which were in New England, mid-Atlantic, and southern states. Lambda at Kenyon College, Gambier, Ohio, and Kappa at Miami University, Oxford, Ohio were west of the Alleghenies, and Omicron was established at the University of Michigan.

Although located outside of DKE's major geographical locations, Kappa contributed to the Fraternity's growth by being the first to be founded in "the West." Students had come to

Miami University from all neighboring states, as well as from the South, logically leading to DKE's presence on campus. Kappa distinguished itself in the university's literary societies, receiving, at one point, more honors than all the other secret organizations combined.

In 1861 Kappa leased from the University two large rooms in a building overlooking the campus, marking the first Greek homestead at Miami, a school renowned for its strong fraternity tradition. A massive doorway impressed initiates with the profound mysteries of the inner temple, and at night the light from inside the building illuminated stained glass windows, exquisitely revealing DKE's arms and other heraldic devices.

"Fraternities are comprised of men who are independent-minded..."

Important though this building was, it was not the earliest –In 1854 Lambda Chapter, at Kenyon College in Gambier, Ohio, as will be seen, built the first fraternity lodge in America. In 1861 the mother chapter Phi built the first college fraternity "tomb" which was used at Yale for over half a century; Omicron at Michigan and Mu at Colgate, built, respectively, the Shant and the Temple in the 1870s.

STEMMING THE TIDE

Along with fraternities, resistance to them grew. Antisecret society sentiment was widespread, but rather than driving fraternities out, the hostility had the opposite effect: the most intelligent and persistent undergraduates found such brotherhoods appealing, either in spite of such opposition, or perhaps, because of it.

With its members possessing high standards of conduct, DKE gained an enviable reputation and gave critics little cause to take action against the Fraternity. Still, for years DKE's chapters were forced to meet secretly in barns, hotels, and the homes of sympathizers. Ironically, secrecy served to fuel chapter independence and strengthen the organization. Dufour Bayle (Tau Lambda, 1955) explained: "Fraternities are comprised of men who are independent-minded, and they don't like to be told how to act or behave. Fraternity men are typically leaders and they are not going to conform."

Scott Kegler (Delta Kappa, 1991) agreed. "There's been a tradition of Deke men who do things a little differently, and that's what makes them successful," he said.

Eventually Mu not only met with opposition but practically invited it.

Rho sent a delegation to Phi in the early fall of 1855, which was well received and resulted in a charter being granted to Rho in October. Installation was done at a local hotel in Philpsburg, NJ, across the river, and subsequent chapter meetings were held on or near the Lafayette campus. For many years Rho's meetings were held at midnight. Members crept out of their rooms at 11:30 p.m. and quietly made their way to rendezvous, ducking into darkened doorways when they heard footsteps. The locations of the chapter meetings were conveyed by a cryptic set of symbols, boldly and publicly displayed on campus, which, however, only Dekes were able to interpret.

Some chapters, such as Mu, had an ongoing debate with faculty. Established at Colgate University, Hamilton, New York, in March 1856, the chapter was more than successful. By spring forty men of the approximately 150 men enrolled at the university had joined. In spite of its popularity among the students, Mu was aware of the school's antifraternity laws and tried to meet discreetly. After ascertaining that the university library was not a "safe" place, members gathered at sympathizers' establishments, such as the Masonic Hall.

Eventually Mu not only met with opposition but practically invited it. Chapter lore credits Caleb H. Gallup (1856) with starting "all the trouble" by openly wearing his DKE pin to commencement exercises, clearly announcing the society's existence on campus. The faculty could not overlook such blatant disregard for the university's laws and initiated an official inquiry the following fall.

The faculty resolved that the law was for the "good of the institution," and it required strict enforcement. It formed a committee to discover the identities of Mu's members. Some Brothers gave in to the pressure and asked to be released from the secret society's membership, but many others braved the wrath of their opponents. Mu was determined to maintain its organization until either the law changed or the Brothers were expelled.

At a meeting between the faculty and Mu, the former hoped to "persuade the members on moral grounds to give up the organization." They offered to forgo disciplinary action against the students as long as the chapter was dissolved. Meanwhile, Mu members proposed a compromise of their own. They would follow all university rules within the organization and police the behavior of all members, and they would not use their influence to gain control of the school's literary societies.

After several rounds of negotiations, the university insisted the chapter disband, requiring that all members sign a pledge not to "re-establish or perpetuate a secret organization." On June 20, 1857, Mu formally dispersed. However, one member, John Ross Baumes, managed to evade signing the pledge, and on graduation night he initiated eight incoming freshmen. Mu survived at Colgate despite the faculty's apparent victory. William Newton Clarke (Mu, 1861) recounted the atmosphere at Colgate in *DKE Quarterly*, Volume 26, Number 3:

> It was an interesting life that we lived in those days. Of course we were under perpetual ban of the law, and we understood it. We had no reason to doubt that the full force of the law would be used against us if we were discovered. . . . By all odds the chapter was to us the most interesting thing in college. It has the savor of mystery and concealment, and it brought a sense of responsibility as well.
>
> The faculty had taught the boys one trick, or suggested it to them. The paper that our predecessors had to sign declared that the chapter had been disbanded: disbanding, then, was all that the faculty asked. Very well, they would disband; and by vote the chapter was disbanded at the close of every meeting, and reorganized when it met again. Between meetings the chapter did not exist.

Unfortunately, not all chapters survived persecution.

Unfortunately, not all chapters survived persecution. DKE's third chapter, Zeta, established at Princeton on September 15, 1845, was forced to disband what had been a very successful group one year after its installation under pressure from the school. Efforts were made to revive it six years later, but the faculty remained adamant and after a five-year struggle, the chapter closed. It was successfully revived in 1987.

Psi from the start was a strong chapter, demonstrating enviable leadership qualities in establishing other chapters. The first fraternity at the University of Alabama, Psi's business was conducted in extreme secrecy for several years. By 1852 Alpha Delta Phi and Phi Gamma Delta fraternities had also established chapters at the university. Opposition to fraternities began to grow, resulting in their banishment in 1856. Nearly thirty years later the ban was lifted and Psi once more became active, and a leading chapter of DKE.

...by the end of the century many chapters had their own houses...

From the Ground Up

At the time of Lambda's installation, Kenyon College was another institution that had enacted a law forbidding secret societies. Yet the West attracted men of great determination, and the men of Lambda Chapter were no exception. The Brothers wasted no time in setting up their new chapter, meeting secretly in an abandoned log hut for several months. The chapter's pride grew until, in 1854, the graduating members openly wore their DKE badges and bravely petitioned the college to remove its unjust law. Faculty members were shocked, but agreed to abolish the antifraternity law if a faculty member were permitted to attend the meetings. Lambda agreed, choosing their own faculty member, and the issue was settled.

Finally able to participate freely in DKE, the young men decided the run-down hut was no longer adequate and set about building their own meeting place, the first fraternity lodge in America. The following description appeared January 1884 in Volume 2 of the *DKE Quarterly*: "The site selected was in a deep ravine, out in the dense woods, whose monarchs towered above the spot in a steep ascent on both sides, and amid a heavy growth of underbrush and hazels. A small stream flowed down the center of the valley, and a beautiful spring gushed from the hillside."

Built on land owned by Kenyon College, the lodge was located a mile from campus. The youths built it themselves, using a five-dollar donation to get started. All told, the edifice cost about fifty dollars to build, and the exercise cemented the chapter's unity. In his ninety-year history of DKE, John Clair Minot described the forty-by-twenty foot, ten-foot-high cabin as follows: "Though of unhewn logs on the outside, it was finished and furnished with such luxuries as the times knew and was used regularly for meetings and social occasions for nearly twenty years."

Five years later in 1861, Phi built DKE's second lodge, the design of which became a model for several other chapters, notably Omicron, Michigan and Mu, Colgate, as well as structures of other fraternities. The forbidding, windowless building became known as the "Tomb" and contained a large assembly hall for major meetings, smaller conference rooms, and an area for dramatic representations. Mystic symbols lent an air of mystery to the building.

The idea of building chapter houses in which members could live did not gain momentum until the 1880s, but by the

TEMPLES TO THE GODDESS

Who builds for self,
Builds only for today.
Who builds for love,
Builds for eternity.

–Frank Robertson Moore (Mu, 1875)
Motto inscribed on the walls of Mu's Temple

1872 was a turning point for Mu, when the members realized that in spite of adamant faculty opposition, it needed a meeting hall. The following five years were spent raising funds for such an endeavor, resulting in the first fraternal structure at Colgate College.

Modeled after the Phi Tomb at Yale, the Deke Temple at Colgate University cost approximately four thousand dollars to build. A plain, brick building with filled-in arches, the Temple has been described as "beautiful in its simplicity." Originally the structure had four windows on either side and a front entrance, but early in the twentieth century an alumni provided funding to brick off the windows and place an iron gate over the entrance to deter vandals.

Temple.

The drastic measures enhanced the hall's mystique and secrecy, but through the years it has continually been attacked by vandals and thieves.

Mu Brothers have been duly proud of their Temple since its construction. In the December 1973 issue of the *DKE Quarterly*, Barry Ridings (Mu, 1974) and Richard Switzer (Mu, 1974) expressed their feelings for the building:

> The faces inside the Temple walls may change, but the spirit of the DKE zeal and passion remains the same. . . . The Temple is the focal point of the entire Mu chapter. . . . The one thing that may not be stolen from the Temple is displayed openly and that is its very existence.

Its function remains the same: it is used for meetings and initiations. As the Colgate campus expanded, the Temple became crowded by neighboring buildings, and in 1994, astonishingly enough, the old historic edifice was jacked up and moved intact to a lot adjacent to the Mu Chapter House, not a single brick being lost. The Temple has been completely renovated due to the efforts of the Mu of DKE Foundation and a massive effort fundraising effort successfully completed under the leadership of John R. Wilson (Mu, 1952).

end of the century many chapters had their own houses while others temporarily rented lodgings. Theta, Pi, Epsilon, Gamma Phi, Delta Chi, Phi Gamma, Omicron, Delta Delta, Gamma, and Theta Zeta all had houses to be envied, while many other chapters were making notable strides in that area.

The Shant

Omicron at the University of Michigan was another leading chapter. Starting up with only seven charter members, its number quickly grew and within a year fifteen more brothers had been initiated. Such growth caused Omicron to change halls three times before the outbreak of the Civil War.

After the conflict, in which thirty Omicron Brothers fought and ten died, the chapter expanded rapidly and again required a lodge. In 1872 chapter members and alumni formed the Omicron Literary Association, a corporation that, according to state law, could purchase real estate and build a chapter house. Fundraising immediately ensued, and three years later the chapter purchased a lot located on East William Avenue, Ann Arbor. Architect William LeBaron Jenney, later known as the "father of the skyscraper," was hired to design the new building, which has been described as Gothic Victorian, eclectic Neo-Gothic, and Neo-Renaissance. The cornerstone was laid in 1878, and by the end of the following year the building was completed. Although the structure itself has changed little since its construction, an exterior eight-foot high brick wall was added in 1901, increasing the building's mysterious appearance. It was used only for late night meetings, the gas-lit interior enhancing the building's eeriness.

For nearly a century, few changes were made to Omicron's hall, known as "The Shant," but a fire there in 1967 caused the chapter to leave campus for a period of time. In 1971 Wilfred V. Casgrain (Omicron, 1918), Detroit industrialist and head of the Omicron Literary Association, spearheaded a fundraising drive that would ensure the future of The Shant. He raised over sixty thousand dollars for the building's renovation, transforming it into a fully air-conditioned and equipped facility.

Meanwhile, Omicron Chapter had secured housing on a separate lot, which eventually resulted in a crushing financial burden for the Omicron Literary Association, owner of both properties. Apprehension grew as the association began to consider selling or leasing The Shant for commercial uses to ease its financial obligations. These fears were eased when, in 1985, the Rampant Lion Foundation, DKE's educational foundation, received a generous bequest from Ellis D. Slater (Omicron, 1917) toward the purchase of the building from the O.L.A. Edward J. Frey (Omicron, 1932) began raising funds to complete the transaction, and by the following year funds had been secured, and the Rampant Lion Foundation became the new owner of the building.

Today the Shant stores and displays the DKE archives as well as relics, historical books, writings, and other educational materials of the Fraternity. It is also the site of the Casgrain Slater Frey educational lecture series, named for the three Deke benefactors, and is the location of summer educational conferences. The future may find The Shant serving as the headquarters for the Rampant Lion Foundation.

The Shant.

COMING TOGETHER

As news of DKE fueled its growth in the mid-1800s, Phi brothers welcomed gratifying widespread enthusiasm for the Brotherhood. Yet they soon realized that communication between sister chapters was not all it could be. So on November 14, 1846, Phi passed the following resolution:

> *Resolved*, that we do consider it expedient to hold a general convention of the fraternities in New Haven, on or before the 25th of December next, for the purpose of promoting the more intimate acquaintance between the members of different chapters and to consult upon other interests.

On December 23, 1846–the last day of the autumn session at Yale–delegates from Bowdoin, Colby, and Amherst met with the entire Phi Chapter in Connecticut. The meeting included orations, social functions, and discussions of problems facing the Fraternity. Although this was the first Delta Kappa Epsilon convention, no record can be found of the proceedings. It was, however, the beginning of a tradition that provides support and direction to all chapters to this day.

...Delta Kappa Epsilon's astonishing growth began to weigh heavily on its parent chapter...

For more than half a decade, Brothers discussed having another convention, but it did not transpire until 1852, six years after the first. Held in July, at Brunswick, Maine, the DKE convention was overshadowed by Bowdoin's semicentennial commencement, and little is known about it. However, it did not adjourn until the participants had set a meeting date for the following year. The parent chapter, Phi, would again host the gathering in New Haven on July 26, 1853.

This next convention also coincided with commencement, but Phi went to great lengths in preparing for it. Notices were sent to all chapters and printed in prominent newspapers throughout the country announcing the Third Convention. The result was a highly successful meeting with six chapters represented by thirty-nine delegates and a large body of active and alumni Brothers. Fraternity business was enthusiastically discussed, including awarding a fifty- to one hundred dollar prize to the best writer on any subject, judging to be by a fraternity committee.

Although benefiting the Fraternity, Delta Kappa Epsilon's astonishing growth began to weigh heavily on its parent chapter, which had been the supreme decision maker for ten years. The Fourth Convention, held January 3, 1855 in Washington DC, shifted some legislative responsibility to the convention. More businesslike than previous meetings, the Washington gathering identified chapter obligations and responsibilities and enacted a method of financial organization.

Meeting every year and a half, the conventions took on an increasingly important role in DKE, serving many functions : they became legislative bodies, forums for lively debate, literary and oratorical competitions, and social occasions where strong friendships were formed. Some were more successful than others, but all were productive. To some confusion, in 1858 the numeration was changed: although it was only the seventh such gathering, that convention became known as the Thirteenth Convention because it occurred during the Fraternity's thirteenth year. Subsequent conventions were numbered accordingly.

By the early 1860s, Delta Kappa Epsilon had become a strong, stable organization. It had weathered the wrath of conservative faculties and immeasurable growing pains, but it would not escape unscathed from the ravages of the Civil War.

CHAPTER 2
UNITED WE STAND

During the years leading to the Civil War, differences between the northern and southern states began to affect DKE. With Brothers both above and below the Mason-Dixon Line, the Fraternity witnessed lively discussions in chapter correspondence and literary exercises regarding the right of states to secede. Yet Dekes from the North and South stood fast in their bond of brotherhood, resulting in the passage of the following resolution at DKE's Fifteenth Convention held in New York City, 1860: "that it is the unanimous wish of the delegates present that the convention for 1862 shall be held with some southern chapter of the Fraternity." It was not to be. In "Our Convention Development," which appeared in Volume 2, October 1883 of the *DKE Quarterly*, Charles H. Beckett (Pi, 1881) described what happened next:

> Many a battle field, and prison-hell and unknown graves, and all the horrors of a bloody war–was their "southern convention" of 1862. For then that awful Civil War broke over us–and we paused dumbfounded–like laborers afield, who turning, fling up their hands when the engulfing cyclone sweeps down upon them. From that struggle–no institution was more radically altered, no class of men figured more grandly, no sentiments rose diviner above the smoke of battles–than our own. Upon the altars of that war our chain was hammered to white heat, consumed by that blighting combustion, and every link scarred and calcinated. It is the saddest, sweetest, and the

grandest song of our history, that another time and page shall tell. But aside from the individual heroes, who returned not even on their shields, think of that galaxy of glorious chapters that became extinct!

WEATHERING THE STORM

On both sides of the battlefield, Dekes proudly Maintained the ideals in which they believed. Southern Brothers fought to preserve their way of life and to protect their homes and families, while northern Brothers fought for their flag and country. The bitter conflict was tragic for the Fraternity. With Brothers volunteering "to a man," all the southern chapters, except for Eta at the University of Virginia, closed. Of a total membership of about 2,500, 817 Dekes fought for the North and 725 for the South–a total of 1542, 162 more than the next two fraternities combined. Eight became major generals and more than 800 attained the rank of captain or above. More Deke Brothers lost their lives than men of any other fraternity. Indeed, no nonmilitary organization had ever made such a showing in this country.

The Fraternity paid a heavy price for its participation in the war.

The first officer slain in the war was Theodore Winthrop (Phi, 1848), who was killed at the battle of Bull Run. A Deke also figured prominently at the end of the conflict. Philip Brent (Zeta, 1859) was the last Confederate commander to surrender, six weeks after Lee's surrender at Appomattox. A Brother later wrote:

> Brotherhoods, political parties, even churches and families, divided, separated, and withdrew into hostile camps. There was Church North and a Church South, but never DKE North and DKE South. The Potomac River was no boundary in Delta Kappa Epsilon. Though men enlisted and fought on different sides, according to their conception of right, yet underneath and behind the battle and slaughter and death, there was something stronger and greater than all the battle and the slaughter and the death. The mighty ennobling sentiment that unites true fraternity men to each other is more powerful and enduring than any of the outbreaks, or passions, or conflicts in the midst of which they find themselves involved.

The Fraternity paid a heavy price for its participation in the war. In the year preceding it, two charters had been granted. One went to Phi Chi Chapter at Rutgers College, the other to Kappa Phi at Troy University. By the end of the struggle, however, thirteen DKE chapters had closed, and those remaining were weakened by "the draining from them of the blood of many of

The Tie That Binds

Perhaps the most stirring account of DKE Brotherhood during the war was written by John Clair Minot (Theta, 1896). The northern soldier mentioned was Lieutenant Edwin S. Rogers of the Thirty-first Regiment, Volunteers of Maine. A native of Patten, Maine, Rogers entered Bowdoin College in the class of 1865 and immediately joined DKE. In his junior year he enlisted in the Union Army. It was at Cold Harbor on June 8, 1864 that Rogers was wounded, only to die a few hours later. Minot never learned the name of the southern Deke.

Brothers In DKE

Upon a southern battlefield the twilight shadows fall;
The clash and roar are ended, and the evening bugles call.
The wearied hosts are resting where the ground is stained with red,
And o'er the plain between them lie the wounded and the dead.

And out upon the sodden field, where the armies fought all day,
There came a group of soldiers who wore the rebel gray.
But peaceful was their mission upon the darkened plain:
They came to save their wounded and lay at rest the slain.

And tenderly their hands performed the work they had to do,
And one among them paused beside a wounded boy in blue,
A Northern lad, with curly hair and eyes of softest brown,
Whose coat of blue was red with blood that trickled slowly down.

A bullet hole was in his breast, and there alone he lay
At night upon the battlefield, and moaned his life away.
The rebel paused beside him, and in the lantern's light
He saw upon the soldier's breast a fair familiar sight.
It was the pin of DKE, the diamond, stars and scroll,
The emblem of a brotherhood that bound them soul to soul.
He raised his hand and quickly tore his coat of gray apart
And showed the wounded soldier a Deke pin o'er his heart.

Then close beside the Yankee dropped the rebel to his knee,
And their hands were clasped together in the grip of DKE.
"I'm from Theta," said the Yankee, and he tried to rise his head;
"I'm from Psi, in Alabama," were the words the rebel said.
"Brothers from the heart forever"—nothing more was left to say,
Though one was clad in Northern blue and one in Southern gray.

But the Northern lad was dying; his voice was faint at best
As he murmured out his messages to "mother and the rest."
And as the rebel soothed him, with his head upon his knee,
He heard him whisper "Bowdoin," and the "Dear old DKE."
And he bandaged up the bosom that was torn by rebel shot;
And bathed the brow with water where the fever fires were hot;
And kissed him for his mother, and breathed a gentle prayer
As the angel's wings were fluttering above them in the air.

And to a lonely country home, far in the heart of Maine,
A letter soon was carried from that southern battle plain.
It told about the conflict, and how he bravely fell
Who was the son and brother in that home beloved so well;
It told the simple story of the night when he had died—
All written by the rebel Deke whom God sent to his side.
And when it all was written, the writer sent within
A little lock of curly hair and a battered diamond pin.
And thirty years have passed away, but these simple relics are
Of all a mother treasures dear, the dearest still by far.

A simple tale and simply told, but true; and I thought it might
Well thrill the hearts of loyal Dekes, so I tell it here to-night.
The Northern soldier's name is found on Bowdoin's honor-roll;
And the names of both are blazoned fair on DKE's scroll.
God bless our noble brotherhood; its past is sweet to hear,
And its grandeur and its glory grow with each succeeding year;
And the story of its heroes shall an inspiration be
To us who proudly wear to-day the pin of DKE.

their best and noblest members." Every chapter in the North and South had members who fought in the war, and all bore the scars long afterward. The killing and bloodshed cut a swath of misery and bitterness that still lingers in the nation as a whole. In the case of DKE, seven chapters never recovered: Delta at South Carolina College, Theta Chi at Union College (New York), Kappa Psi at Cumberland University (Tennessee), Tau Delta at Union

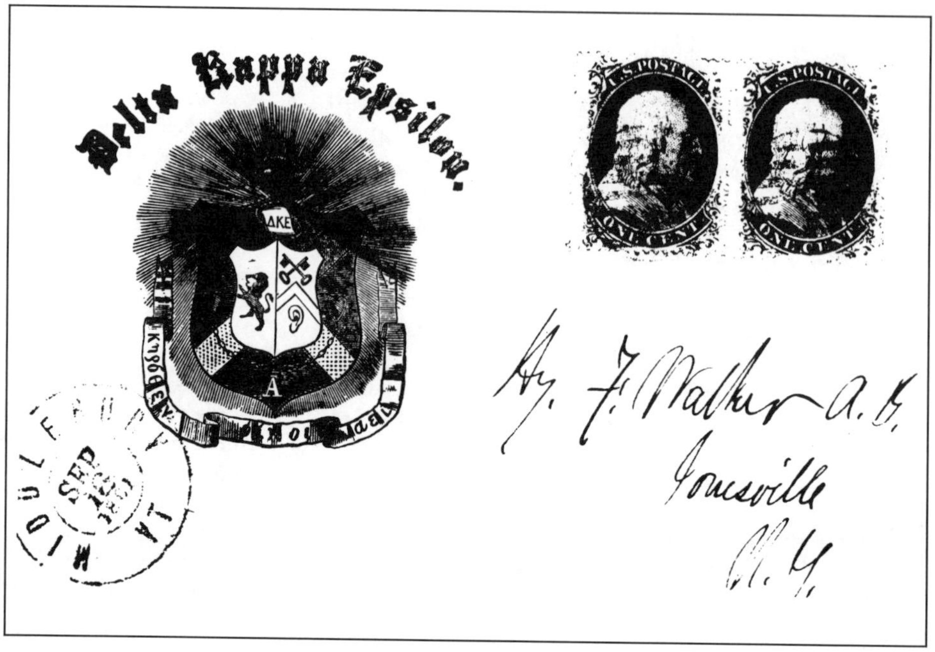

Letter mailed from Middlebury, VT, September 16, 1861.

University (Tennessee), Omega at Oakland College (Mississippi), Alpha Delta at Jefferson College(Pennsylvania), and Kappa Phi at Troy University (New York). The previously vigorous and expanding Brotherhood was , like the country itself, crippled by the ravages of war.

Strengthening the Bonds of Brotherhood

By the end of the conflict Phi had transferred most of the governing responsibilities to the conventions, reasoning that the gatherings were a more appropriate forum for legislative actions. This way, members throughout the Fraternity could participate in policy decisions. Although regular conventions had been held during the war, little business had been transacted.

After the war DKE attempted to dress up its wounds. Healing would be slow, with chapters decimated and colleges extinguished. At the 1865 convention, at which only six chapters were present, a resolution was passionately passed that would reaffirm Delta Kappa Epsilon's unity and begin the healing process:

> *Resolved,* that we, as a convention, rejoice at the restored political and civil relations of our common government, and that we welcome back with undiminished regard the Southern Chapters of our Fraternity, and earnestly desire

> and request that they renew their former relations with the Fraternity at the earliest possible moment.

Although the war left the Fraternity a fraction of its former self, DKE chose to proceed cautiously, strengthening remaining chapters instead of rapidly expanding. Applications for charters were carefully and thoroughly considered at conventions and were usually declined unless the most compelling reasons for approval were found.

The 1866 convention was a memorable one, despite a low turnout. Chi Chapter at the University of Mississippi, Oxford, Mississippi, made her first appearance since before the war, reclaiming her rightful place in DKE and establishing herself as the first southern chapter to return. DKE was pleased to welcome Chi, formally recognizing the delegate in a resolution that also encouraged other southern chapters to rejoin as soon as they could. Charters were granted to Indiana Asbury University and Weseleyan University, the first since before the war, and Phi was instructed to issue a catalogue during the coming year.

Although Phi was no longer the supreme leader of DKE, her position as the mother chapter was held in proper esteem by the other chapters; so when Phi called a special convention in January 1867, they gathered to hear her message. Ten northern chapters listened as Phi revealed her concern: Northern chapters needed strengthening, and whole southern chapters needed rebuilding. The convention closed with the following words:

> Please accept for yourselves and convey to all our brethren you may meet our sincere wish that all the unpleasant occurrences of the past be buried in oblivion, and that we, one and all, both in the South and in the North, stand shoulder to shoulder, hand joined in hand, in the endeavor to push our loved Fraternity to the acme of glory, and show to all the world our fidelity to our motto, "Always friends at heart."

...by 1868 DKE once again had twenty chapters.

Phi's earnest request motivated the rest of the Fraternity and by 1868 DKE once again had twenty chapters. No increase occurred at that year's convention , despite the grant of a charter to Beta Chi at the Western Reserve University, because Theta Chi at Union College, devastated by the war, saw their charter withdrawn.

Growth in the Aftermath

Countless charter applications testified to the high esteem in which DKE was held on campuses throughout the nation. A petition from one institution in particular, Cornell University in Ithaca, New York, immediately drew the attention of the Fraternity. A committee was formed to investigate, and submitted a resoundingly positive report; by the 1870 convention, Delta Chi had been installed and its enthusiastic brothers volunteered to host the Twenty-fifth Convention.

Conservatism reigned at the next two conventions...

The offer was made more out of excitement than practicality. The exuberant chapter members had neither the finances nor the facilities to pull off such an event, but they were determined to make the Convention a success. They rented and furnished suitable chapter rooms, taxing their members about $125 (an enormous sum in 1871) each to cover the cost. Delta Chi Brothers eagerly anticipated showing DKE how dedicated they were, as well as letting the seven other fraternities on campus know that they had arrived.

Just as preparations were being completed, however, the hotel in which the banquet was to be held burned to the ground. With heavy hearts, the chapter members asked university authorities for the use of a reception room on campus. Eventually, the officials acquiesced. The convention was a success, with a large attendance and brilliant orations. The conservative expansion plan remained intact, and only one charter was granted, to Phi Gamma at Syracuse University.

Conservatism reigned at the next two conventions, resulting in no new charter approvals and ten withdrawals from chapters that had been dormant since the war. Yet advancements were made in other areas. Alumni were becoming more involved with the chapters, and a proposal was made to further organize the graduate Dekes. Because the New York area had the largest number of DKE alumni, enthusiasm for stronger alumni associations spread from there to other large cities, and before long DKE had the largest and most organized alumni associations or any fraternity.

The Twenty-eighth Convention, held in October 1874 in Charlottesville, Virginia, was a cause for southern celebration. For the first time, Brothers in the South hosted the gathering. Though the trek was long and expensive for many delegates, the previous convention had determined the need to emphasize

DKE's support for its southern chapters. The decision proved to be a wise one, and nineteen chapters were represented. The members conducted noteworthy business, including the installation of a new chapter, Beta Gamma at Columbia University, New York, but southern hospitality overwhelmed many Brothers who thereafter had cloudy memories at best. One Brother later wrote:

> I was there, to that I'll swear, and so was Bayard Taylor, and to me he was the convention! I distinctly remember that the representative of our chapter was honored with a seat in the same carriage with the aforesaid 'B.T.' during the convention drive to Monticello, where we were photographed on the steps of the old home of Jefferson, Monticello. I also remember that next to "me and Taylor," one other form in that historic group challenged the attention of all, viz.—a demijohn of whiskey!—pronounced good by all the boys, who with rare medical foresight, carried it along as a prophylactic against sunstroke; and as an eyewitness I am willing to affirm that never a son was struck!
>
> As to the business sessions of the convention, although I distinctly remember that on my return my chapter report was accepted as clear, definite and satisfactory, I am now obliged to record with shame the fact that I can't remember a single thing that was done or who did it. I think the oration and poem were the best ever provided for a similar occasion; that the chairman resided with much more than usual dignity; that the banquet was the best on record, the toastmaster unusually felicitous in his remarks, and the responses to the toasts ditto; but I know Bayard Taylor was there, and his stories, inimitably told, threw stacks of fun into the occasion. . . . In fact, he was the jolliest one of the crowd.

The conservative path took a radical turn in 1876...

Bayard Taylor, an honorary member of Omicron, was an author and journalist. He wrote "El Dorado," "Journey to Central Africa," "The Lands of the Saracen," "Northern Travel," "Centennial Ode," "By-ways of Europe" and numerous others. He died December 19, 1878, Berlin, Germany.

The conservative path took a radical turn in 1876 when the delegates of the Thirtieth Convention ruled that the University of California at Berkeley was worthy of a chapter. The step lent validity to DKE's claim of being a national fraternity and fueled an expansion debate. Many Brothers were convinced that DKE should be a fixture on every fine university throughout the country, and those chapters outside the realm of New England and the mid-Atlantic states welcomed the idea of new neighbors. Nevertheless, Delta Kappa Epsilon stayed its conservative course, granting only one charter and reviving two.

Though few charters had been granted since the war, DKE's stability grew. The Brotherhood recognized the need to develop closer contact with chapters and to address the needs of the fraternity as a whole. As the 1880s drew closer, DKE prepared to enter a significant new era.

CHAPTER 3

A DEMOCRACY DEVELOPS

The early 1880s brought further prestige to the already celebrated Fraternity. On March 4, 1881, after a successful administration in which he accomplished the rare Presidential feat of leaving office more popular than when he entered it, Rutherford B. Hayes handed over the presidency of the United States of America to James A. Garfield. To the great delight of his Brothers, Hayes, a Deke, was the first member of a fraternity to become president. The Brotherhood was proud to see one of its own in the White House, paving the way for future Deke leaders.

SHARING THE RESPONSIBILITY

During this time, DKE's careful growth was strong and steady. Young men throughout the nation sought to join the quality organization that offered them brotherhood and personal encouragement. With the spreading enthusiasm, however, came growing pains. Chapters were operating on their own, for the most part, meeting for conventions and following the basic principles of the Fraternity, but overall organization was lacking. Yearly gatherings were not enough to unite the growing Fraternity, and the chapter members could little afford to be further taxed to finance convention expenses and their own needs. Still, the active undergraduates realized that cooperation among the chapters required more continuous attention than correspondence and conventions could give them.

And so the Council of Alumni...was established, providing chapters with a new source of information...

These frustrations were given a voice by the delegates of the Thirtieth Convention, at which a committee was formed to address organizational options. Two years later, the committee, chaired by Frank S. Williams (Nu, 1878) proposed dividing the Fraternity into three segments with headquarters in Boston, New York, and Detroit. The first section would consist of the New England states; the second would include New York, New Jersey, Pennsylvania, and Virginia; while the third section would encompass those areas not covered by the other two. Each chapter would have a councilor in its own section, and Phi would have a councilor in all sections. The convention adopted the plan, but its complexity led to a lack of support among chapters and it was never ratified.

At the Thirty-fifth Convention in 1881, Henry W. Rolfe (Sigma, 1880) brought forth another, simpler, plan for centralized government involving one council of alumni, located in New York. The concept appealed to the chapters and was passed. Five alumni, living in or near New York, were elected by the convention to serve two-year terms, with assistance from a professional, paid secretary. The secretary would serve a key role by maintaining contact with the chapters and reporting important information to the Council.

And so the Council of Alumni, acting as executive of the Fraternity, was established, providing chapters with a new source of information and assistance. The Council was empowered to supervise the Fraternity catalogue and magazine, receive all applications for charters, report on those applications at conventions, and take care of other administrative duties. A fund was set up to cover the Council's expenses, but the councilors themselves volunteered their time.

Due to increased communication by the Council with all the chapters and its addressing of the needs of the Fraternity as a whole, DKE flourished. In the *History of the Fraternity,* Aldice Warren (Beta Phi, 1883), sang the praises of the Council:

> To those who have never felt the thrill which leaps from heart to heart through the hands clasped in the Mystic Circle, it is inexplicable how men engrossed in the daily toil of business, of the professions, of politics, can be willing to give up so much of their time and labor, without recompense, simply to promote the interests of an organization of college boys, whose principal object to the uninitiate seems to be to have a good time, and to shroud that good time in a certain mystery. These barbarians little realize the love which binds

Developing a Coat of Arms

Heraldry has been used since the Middle Ages when armorial devices emblazoned on their shields were used by armour-clad warriors as forms of identification. When DKE was in its infancy the founders adopted an heraldic crest in crimson, blue, and gold (referred to as *gules, azure,* and *or* in the preferred French description of heraldry), the design of which was published on facing page three in the first catalogue in 1851. After the Council was formed, a general system of chapter heraldry was devised, in a large part due to Franklin W. Lantz (Psi Phi, 1870). He explained later, in an article for Volume 3 of the *DKE Quarterly,* that the arms chosen by the founders were largely symbolic, "the heart of *gules* linked by the chain of *or,* the chevrons countrepointed, the radiated eye in chief, the escutcheon of pretense with its combined shields, the winged globe cresting the achievement. *Arma inquirenda,* too they made them. For was not a new kingdom founded when DKE was established?"

Everything contained within DKE's heraldry has meaning. The symbols, colors, and even the arrangement of the devices are symbolic. Lantz described it in heraldic terms in his article:

> **Arms.** Azure, between two chevrons counterpoint, the superior or, the inferior gules, as many hearts of the last, issuing thereout a chain pendant over all, the link in the base point in form of a Greek letter Phi, of the second; in chief an eye proper, radiated *or;* and upon an escutcheon in pretense, argent, a lion rampant sable, langued gules, impaling argent, a chevron between two keys endorsed in saltier in chief sable, and in base three mullets, two and one, in form of a triple star, *gules, azure, or.*
>
> **Crest.** A globe, or winged argent.
>
> **Motto.** *Kerothen Philoi' Aei,* "Friends from the Heart, Forever."

The nature of DKE's symbolism is revealed only to Brothers at their initiation.

Each chapter also has a crest, based in part on the DKE crest, but with its own design and motto.

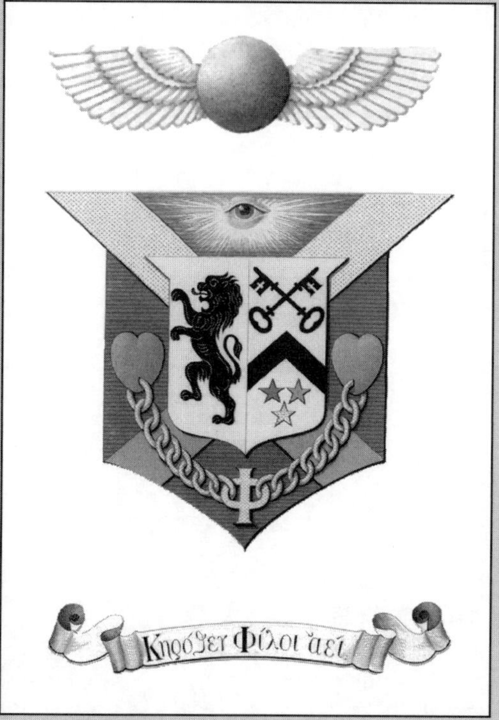

the true Greek to his fraternity with a bond which grows stronger as the years advance. The members of our Council have been men of prominence in their various callings, whose advice is eagerly sought for, and commands a high price in this busiest of cities; yet they have freely given of their time to the work of the Fraternity, and much of her progress is due to their wisdom and foresight. Nothing has been left to chance by them.

The first Council members were Frank S. Williams (Nu, 1878), president; John DeWitt Warner (Delta Chi, 1872), secretary; and Dickinson W. Richards (Phi, 1880), G. A. Plimpton (Sigma, 1876), and Charles H. Beckett (Pi, 1881) as representatives. In March

A Singing Fraternity

Since its inception, DKE has been a musical fraternity and in its 150-year history has had its share of well-known musicians. Cole Porter (Phi, 1913) filled the world with unforgettable songs, including "What Is This Thing Called Love?" "Night and Day," "Anything Goes," and "It's De-Lovely." And in the 1950s Richard W. "Dick" Clark (Phi Gamma, 1951) became a household name as "American Bandstand" began its thirty-year reign on television. William T. Purdy (Tau, 1906) composed many college songs, including the rousing "On Wisconsin." And another Phi Deke, class of 1898, Charles Ives, is one of the great names in the world of modern classical music.

Yet DKE did not merely listen to the music of a notable few. Music is an important part of Fraternity functions. DKE's first songbook appeared in 1857 - decades before its first magazine–and contained songs written by members to celebrate "the glories of the Fraternity and to sing its praises."

In 1871 a larger songbook was produced, containing 154 songs and their accompanying music. This widely popular edition was so comprehensive that no other was published until the turn of the century, when the 1900 edition appeared, containing one hundred of the previous publication's songs and a number of new ones. A second edition was printed in 1907. As the Fraternity grew, tunes used for DKE songs began to vary from chapter to chapter. In 1959 DKE produced a long-playing record "The Songs of DKE" featuring a dozen popular Fraternity standards professionally recorded, and, subsequently, a tape cassette.

Cole Porter, Phi (1913).

David Easlick, (Omicron , 1969) and Dick Clark (Phi Gamma, 1951) present Lou Bantle (Phi Gamma, 1951), Chairman UST with award at Syracuse Homecoming. Also pictured, Carmen Davoli (Phi Gamma, 1962).

1882 they addressed such activities as collecting Fraternity annals, issuing magazines and catalogues, and setting up an alumni club. The Council also wanted a clear picture of what Delta Kappa Epsilon needed to keep it strong and cohesive. Accordingly, chapters were surveyed on a number of questions relating to their colleges, internal affairs, memberships, rites and ceremonies, financial conditions, and relationships with other chapters.

With this information in hand, the Council made its recommendations to the 1882 convention: it suggested adopting a system of heraldry, eliminating chapter debts, and publishing a yearbook, and making some organizational improvements. The convention adopted the proposals with few changes.

No man, no matter now valuable his contribution, was deemed more important than the Fraternity.

By 1883 the Council had met most of those goals and began working on others. They had issued the first volume of the *DKE Quarterly*, prepared and published in color the coat-of-arms of the Fraternity, started a library that included college and fraternity publications, and made substantial progress on a catalogue. The Council also began revising the DKE Constitution, and in 1884 it became the Incorporated Fraternity of Delta Kappa Epsilon, acting under a charter granted by the State of New York.

The Council's work further invigorated DKE, and within ten years three chapters, Gamma at the University of Nashville, Psi at University of Alabama, and Beta Alpha at the University of North Carolina, were revived, a charter was granted to Phi Epsilon at the University of Minnesota, thirteen alumni associations were organized, and a catalogue of all active Fraternity members was finally published.

One reason for the Council's rapid success lay in the principle of rotation, which had been carefully stipulated in the DKE Constitution. No man, no matter how valuable his contribution, was deemed more important than the Fraternity. Regardless of the importance of his ideas or plans, when a member's term in office expired, he knew he must yield to his successor, and that man would either continue the plans, or, at his discretion, change them. This infused the Council with a constant flow of new energy and ideas, fueling the continued success of the Council and the Fraternity.

In 1910, several changes took place in the Council. The first enlarged the alumni representation to nine, and the second required monthly meetings. Use of the phrase, "Once a Deke, always a Deke," was encouraged, expressing the importance of alumni in the Fraternity. They had become an integral part of the Brotherhood, with chapters depending on them for financial, intellectual, and moral support.

A Commitment For Life

Though efforts had been made to organize alumni associations in the past—most notably at the Twenty-seventh Convention, when James I. Good (Rho, 1872) introduced a resolution directing alumni to organize in larger cities—it was only after the formation of the Council that real strides were made. Encouraging the development of alumni societies was a primary goal for the newly elected Council, and the best example was the DKE Club of New York City, an alumni association that offered support and hospitality to visiting and local Dekes. The DKE Club of New York was built on the enthusiasm of the alumni and incorporated under the laws of the state. Members from anywhere in the nation could find fellowship there, and it was an appropriate place for the councilors to meet.

Yale Club of New York City, current site of the DKE CLUB.

Although the Council had successfully recommended an alumni club to the convention in 1882, the organization was not officially established until 1885. The plans were formally announced by Councilor Frank Williams to more than three hundred alumni at a dinner at Delmonico's on February 6. Fraternal enthusiasm was widespread, and by the end of the evening numerous membership applications had been submitted. On May 1, 1885, the DKE Club of New York opened its clubhouse at 36 West Thirty-fourth Street with a burgeoning roll of 250 members. Charlton T. Lewis (Phi, 1853) was named president.

The organization quickly outgrew its first clubhouse and moved to 435 Fifth Avenue, where it became the center of Fraternity activities. The new location housed a cafe, offices, meeting rooms, a banquet hall, and quarters for visiting Dekes.

The DKE Club of New York was initially successful, but changing times began to challenge it. As various large college clubs began cropping up in the early 1900s, competing with the smaller fraternity clubs. The DKE Club temporarily closed, but the alumni quickly reorganized, creating the

Delta Kappa Epsilon Association of New York in 1904. Still referred to as the DKE Club, it moved seven times in its first fifty years, finally establishing a permanent clubhouse and General Fraternity headquarters at the Yale Club, 50 Vanderbilt Avenue in New York City. The twenty-three-story building houses several restaurants and bars, a pool, a gym, squash courts, a library, meeting rooms, barber shops and other services, and ten floors of guest bedrooms. Membership to this exclusive private club is not automatic to all Dekes, however. A Brother must be nominated by one club member, with another "seconding" the motion. "Belonging to the DKE Club is one of the greatest privileges that any Deke can have," said Charles Blaisdell (Pi, 1937). "After a Deke graduates from college, he can become a member of the DKE Club. It will give him an unlimited amount of professional and economic help and social prestige."

DKE was a living, breathing entity, continually changing...

In an article in The *DKE Quarterly* published at the time of The DKE Club Centennial in 1986, Editor and past Chairman, Duncan Andrews, Rho 1957 wrote:

> The DKE Club has not survived by accident. It has survived because, ultimately, enough good men decided to keep a good thing going. It has been affected by history, and not always beneficially, but, at least within DKE, it has made history, too. In a changing world it has been to many Dekes both a symbol and a concrete example of the enduring friendship and companionship that characterize Delta Kappa Epsilon, and the good times that, often against odds, Dekes manage to have.

The Name Game

While the Council dutifully set out to organize the present and document the past, the Fraternity continued to address other issues. DKE was a living, breathing entity, continually changing with the ebb and flow of chapter activity. Though the heart of DKE was perpetually strong, chapters could not always maintain their own involvement, and periods of dormancy were not uncommon.

The revival of the old Beta Chapter at the University of North Carolina was an important issue at the Fortieth Convention, held on January 5 and 6, 1887. The Fraternity knew very little about chapter reorganization efforts in the South, but Professor F.P. Venable (Eta, 1874), Hon. Henry R. Shorter (Beta, 1853), and Judge Alfred B. Irion (Beta, 1855) articulately and passionately described the keen desire of Beta and other chapters

The DKE Catalogue

During the years immediately following its creation, the young Council faced another challenge: producing a Fraternity catalogue. Others had been published, but DKE was in need of an updated version. The first one, compiled in 1851, contained names and addresses of Dekes. Comparable to other fraternity catalogues of the time, an updated version of 1857 was much like its predecessor. The first catalogue to contain biographical information was published in 1874, but it was a modest production compared to that of 1890.

The 1890 Catalogue, the project was a huge undertaking in both manpower and expense, taking more than three years to complete and costing several thousand dollars. At first, the Council underestimated the amount of work the catalogue would require. Surely, they, the chapters had kept accurate records of all their members and would supply these for the effort. Collecting the information, however, was no simple feat for editor Hervey Van Alen Anderson (Gamma Beta, 1884). The Fraternity's history stretched over forty years, and chapter records were disappointingly sketchy and inaccurate. In the South, many records had been destroyed during the Civil War. In every chapter there were numerous members of whom little or nothing was known, and tracing them proved almost impossible. Most of the information on the more than ten thousand members had to be gathered through personal correspondence. Anderson determinedly and faithfully toiled over the publication, though his health failed him. Sadly, he died before he could see the fruits of his labor.

The next editor, George E. Fisher (Beta Phi, 1868) faced an even larger task. He found that much of the previously compiled information was incomplete and he loyally dedicated his time to creating a "monumental work in accuracy, in details, in the information given, and in workmanship." The work would chart the Fraternity's growth along with members' honors in all facets of life.

That edition of the *Catalogue of Delta Kappa Epsilon* far surpassed anything ever done by any fraternity at the time, and DKE has not published another on such a grand scale. It contained a biographical sketch of every member, living and dead, including college and post-graduate honors, changes of residence, publications, travel, and much, much more. The biographies were supplemented by geographical distribution of members, family ties, and service records. The men of inactive chapters were not overlooked, either. Aldice Warren explained in 1890 of the *DKE Quarterly*: "The causes which made so many of our southern chapters inactive—dead they can never be—reflect no dishonor on DKE, and the illustrious names of good and brave men which appear on their rolls ought never to be forgotten."

to revive their bonds with DKE. Many Brothers were moved to tears when the three pleaded the cause of southern institutions. When the vote was finally taken, all delegates were in favor of reestablishing the chapter, and a new focus was made on reviving chapters in the South.

The issue of reestablishing a chapter at the University of North Carolina was far simpler than deciding what to call it, however. The Civil War had extinguished many southern colleges and universities and with them DKE chapters. As DKE chapters were installed in the North, some were given names that had been previously used in the South. Beta was an example. The chapter at Columbia University had served the Fraternity well under that name and did not relish giving it up. The two chapters agreed upon a compromise: the North Carolina chapter became Beta Alpha, though reluctantly. In 1887 Beta Alpha again expressed displeasure at being assigned a new name and Columbia eventually conceded, becoming Gamma Beta.

Chapter Crests from DKE QUARTERLY, 1887.

Inactive southern chapters were not the only ones to suffer this confusion. In fact, Harvard had experienced it twice. That chapter had originally been called Gamma after the University of Nashville chapter had become inactive. When the Nashville chapter reactivated, the Harvard chapter was given the name Alpha. In 1857 Harvard became inactive, and her name was given to a new chapter at Middlebury College in Vermont. When Harvard reestablished its chapter in 1860, Middlebury became known as Alpha Prime, which later was changed to Alpha Alpha.

Half a Century of Brotherhood

DKE turned fifty in 1894, and the celebration was not just of her age but also her accomplishments. Thirty-five chapters dotted the nation, nineteen with their own chapter houses. Twenty-two alumni associations had been formed, and more than ten thousand names graced the DKE rolls. The Brotherhood was "preeminently one of bench and bar," according to Judge Isaac Newton Mills (Sigma, 1874), who noted that, according to the *DKE Catalogue*, more members had been in legal professions than any other field, with 2,432 Dekes serving as lawyers, approximately one-fifth of whom became judges. The next highest concentration of Deke professionals was 877 clergymen.

The Semicentennial Convention, hosted by the Council in New York City, was a tribute to the Brotherhood's success.

Tiffany loving cup presented to William Boyd Jacobs in 1894 now serves as the LION TROPHY.

Attendance surpassed all other conventions to that date. The presence of the last living founder, William Boyd Jacobs, lent an air of reverence to the celebration. For him, it was a bittersweet occasion. He was overjoyed by DKE's success but saddened that he was the only founder left to see the society turn fifty. At the banquet, he reflected on DKE's history and the changes he had witnessed, pointing out the contrast of the organization's modest beginning at Yale with the "magnificent display in this Convention of the healthy and vigorous growth of our beloved Fraternity." He was awestruck by the phenomenal growth of the society he helped start. The convention members listened raptly as this wise leader gave them his message and advice for the future:

> Go forward. The future is yours. What it contains we cannot know now. But be very sure of this, that if—as you cannot fail to do, I am sure—you live up to the meaning indicated by your title DKE, while you will find your future brightened by many joys and pleasures, the chief of which will be the consciousness of duties done and triumphs won, you may also meet with the shadows of disappointments and sorrows, until, having met all bravely and loyally, in accordance with the teachings of DKE, you too shall be carried to your rest with the answer to the roll-call in your surviving comrades' hearts, "died on the field of honor." Be faithful and true while you are here to the honor and interests of our beloved Fraternity. It is yours to press forward.

On behalf of all the chapters, toastmaster Charlton T. Lewis (Phi, 1853) presented Jacobs with a handsome loving cup. The crowd's cheers lasted fifteen minutes. Jacobs made a presentation of his own when he donated his original DKE pin, which he had worn over his heart for fifty years, to the DKE Club of New York, in custody for the Fraternity. At Brother Jacob's death in 1905 his silver Tiffany trophy was returned to the Fraternity by his daughter, and is now symbolically presented each year to the chapter judged to be the best in overall performance. The Lion Trophy is DKE's highest chapter award.

The editor of the *DKE Quarterly* summed up the society's success when he wrote, "The first half century is past. For fifty years has DKE existed, with the fiftieth year the most prosperous of them all. Hers has been a steady, lasting growth. May we not hope that the next half century will see the record of the past upheld."

Harvard Loses DKE

From the beginning Alpha Chapter differed from all the other DKE chapters as Harvard men were allowed to join DKE as sophomores and another fraternity, Alpha Delta Phi, as juniors. This dual membership policy was always a problem for DKE. Phi had determined in 1851 that Harvard was worthy of the Brotherhood, but the ability of its men to loyally serve more than one Greek letter society at the same time was questioned. Through the early years Harvard Brothers seemed as loyal as those of any other chapter. Yet as time went on, Alpha participated less and less Fraternity in activities. Delegates rarely attended the conventions, and visiting Dekes often went unrecognized at Harvard. Yet the chapter had produced many loyal alumni including J. Pierpont Morgan, Theodore Roosevelt, Owen Wister, Henry Cabot Lodge, and Robert Todd Lincoln, whose feelings were important to the Brotherhood. At the 1889 convention, delegates from throughout the nation expressed their frustration with the Alpha situation.

The committee assigned to investigate Alpha brought back a negative report, yet withdrawing Harvard's charter was a difficult decision. The chapter's large and influential body of alumni and the university's status as one of the finest institutions in the country were important considerations. Still, Alpha's recent record left the Fraternity little hope that things would change. The announcement of Alpha's charter withdrawal was made with regret in 1891, after years of debate. The remnants of DKE at Harvard continued as the infamous "Dicky" Club until into the 1960s. These men initiated into the "DKE" included President Franklin D. Roosevelt and Ambassador Joseph Kennedy. The chapter itself remained inactive for one hundred years, and was finally reestablished on April 28, 1991.

DKE was destined to remain in Boston, however, it granted a charter to Sigma Tau at Massachusetts Institute of Technology the same year Alpha closed, and the new chapter quickly became a valued asset to the Fraternity.

The century was drawing to a close, and it looked as though the fraternity would continue adding to its membership...

A Badge of Honor

As the end of the century drew near, DKE commemorated its continued success in 1897 by adopting a new pin modeled after the original DKE badge worn so proudly by Brother Jacobs. In the past, individual initiates had been allowed to specify the size and jeweling of their pins, which led to an eclectic collection of large and small pins adorned with scrollwork, pearls or gems of the chapters' or member's choosing. There was no consistency, and it was occasionally difficult to determine that the wearer actually belonged to the Delta Kappa Epsilon Fraternity. Chapters were also permitted to have their chapter name or Greek letter(s) on the face of the pin.

The new pin, of the same design of the original of 1844 but slightly smaller in size and without any chapter designation (except for Mother Phi, whose pins continue to bear the word "Yale"), was protected by a patent, and the right to manufacture was given to "a competent jeweler who maintained its excellence," according to the 1910 *Catalogue of DKE*. Since the pins were numbered, the DKE Secretary had records of their owners. If one was lost and subsequently returned to the Council—which happened–the secretary checked the number on the back, referred to his records, and forwarded the pin to its rightful owner. The new regulation pin cost four dollars including engraving and mailing charges. All undergraduates were obligated to purchase it and persuade graduate members to do the same.

Leading the Nation to Victory

The century was drawing to a close, and it looked as though the fraternity would continue adding to its membership and reinforcing its existing chapters. However, high hopes for the new century were temporarily dimmed when the Spanish-American War broke out in April 1898. The stir was in large part due to pro-war sentiment published in William Randolph Hearst's newspapers. Hearst, a Harvard Deke, and Joseph Pulitzer published sensational accounts of Spanish oppression in Cuba and claimed that a quarter of the population had died. Americans were outraged by these accounts and demanded U.S. intervention. The battleship *Maine* was blown up in Havana harbor on February 15, 1898, killing 260 people, among them J. Frank Aldrich (Psi Omega, 1877), who had just been appointed U.S. consul general to Havana.

Again proving their patriotism and loyalty, Dekes played prominent roles in the Spanish-American War. The last minister to Spain before the war, Stewart L. Woodford (Phi, 1854), was a Deke, as was the first minister to Spain after the war, Bellamy Storer (Alpha, 1867). The first American officer to die during the war was Rutgers Deke John B. Gibbs (Phi Chi, 1878), a surgeon in the army in the Philippines. And of course there was Theodore Roosevelt (Alpha, 1880), the former New York City police commissioner who resigned his position as the assistant secretary of the navy and formed the Rough Riders, a volunteer cavalry group with which he charged up Cuba's San Juan Hill and eventually, into the Presidency.

Whitelaw Reid (Kappa, 1856).

Senator Henry Cabot Lodge, another Alpha Deke, proposed accepting Spain's surrender, and one of the peace treaty negotiators was Whitelaw Reid (Kappa, 1856), who had been a U.S. Ambassador to France and subsequently served as Ambassador to Great Britain.

Though the Spanish-American War centered on the liberation of Cuba, it also marked the emergence of the United States as a world power. When the war was over, the United States had won Guam, Puerto Rico, and the Philippine Islands; it was no longer an isolated geographic entity, but had, like its older European counterparts, taken on the trappings of empire.

At the end of the war, the Fraternity formed the DKE Association of the Philippines on November 30, 1898, at a meeting held at the Cafe de Paris in Manila. Nine Dekes were present, representing eight different chapters. Phi sent the oldest delegate, Major Robert Hughes Fitzhugh (Phi, 1861), who was elected president of the association. Stories were exchanged, Deke songs sung, and friendships cemented, while wide-eyed waiters looked on in wonder and delight.

Thus Delta Kappa Epsilon ended the century with hope, prosperity, accomplishment, and growth. With the Fraternity boasting thirty-seven chapters, an organization in the South Pacific, and most U.S. chapters living in their own houses, the future seemed bright and secure. The coming century would hold new challenges, new hopes, and new visions, for the Nation, and for Delta Kappa Epsilon.

Chapter 4

Exploring New Frontiers

The 1900s emerged with Dekes at the forefront. Six months after his inauguration in 1901, President William McKinley was assassinated, putting a youthful Theodore Roosevelt in the Oval Office. A self-proclaimed friend of labor, the forty-three-year-old Deke worked for an amicable relationship between government, business, and labor unions and was instrumental in breaking the stranglehold many monopolies had on competition throughout the nation. "Speak softly and carry a big stick" epitomized his foreign policy, and he made notable strides in conservation. In 1904 his dedication and determination won him another term in office. After Roosevelt died in 1919, Major-General Leonard Wood M.D. (Alpha, 1884), remembered the man he had commanded in the Spanish-American War:

> He perhaps more than any man in public life appreciated that true democracy means equality not only of opportunity and privilege but also of obligation; that there can be no true democracy which does not welcome honest criticism and practice frank and fearless publicity. No one knew better than he that a democracy shunning publicity, resenting criticism and striving to limit free expression of opinion on the part of press or people, is a democracy in danger, if not a democracy dying.
>
> His voice has been raised on many issues, sometimes in commendation, sometimes in criticism, but always with a

Autographed photograph of Theodore Roosevelt which hangs in the Delta Kappa House at the University of Pennsylvania.

purpose single to the people's welfare. He hated shams, was intolerant of weakness and feared nothing so much as failure to do his whole duty as he saw it. Many people misjudged him, but no one who knew him intimately ever failed to recognize that, right or wrong, his desire was for the good of our people and the upholding of sound national policy.

The President of the United States was not the only Deke in the national spotlight. Owen Wister (Alpha, 1882) wrote *The Virginian,* a novel that became 1902's best seller and remained popular for decades. The quote "When you call me that, smile!"

became a household phrase. The book, the prototype of the modern Western novel, was dedicated to Wister's friend and fellow Alpha Deke, Theodore Roosevelt.

Carrie Nation: longtime suffragette and anti-liquor crusader.

Not all Dekes were national names, yet DKE cherished their accomplishments. The Brotherhood paid close attention to the 1905 governor's race in Rhode Island as two members of the same chapter, Sigma at Amherst, faced off in the contest. Democrat Lucius F.C. Garvin (Sigma, 1862), who had been governor for the two previous years, was defeated by Republican George H. Utter (Sigma, 1877). The 1905 *DKE Quarterly* described the way the race was run: "Both are extremely popular men, and the fight was waged with the best of feeling between them."

What has been described as the "ultimate fraternity prank" was pulled off by members of the Phi Chapter in 1903. Carrie Nation, longtime suffragette and anti liquor crusader came to New Haven to give a speech. Posing as reporters for the *Yale Daily News*, members of the Class of 1905 lured her to a hotel room and set up a pose for the photographer. Ms. Nation was asked to hold a glass of water so that the photographer could get a proper reflection and then told that the lights needed to be doused for the flash. When the lights went out, the DKEs pulled pipes and flasks from under their coats and the resulting picture appears to feature Carrie Nation drinking and smoking at a wild fraternity party.

There were also sad moments for DKE in the early years of the twentieth century. Many celebrated Brothers died, including founder William Jacobs, who passed away on March 30, 1905.

Coming of Age

With such leaders to call Brothers, there is little wonder why DKE's popularity among young collegians surged. Beginning in the late 1800s, chapter application flooded the Council, touching off a major debate within the Fraternity. Many members believed DKE needed to become more progressive in her expansion efforts. In Volume 18, Number 3, November, 1900, of the *DKE Quarterly,* Samuel E. Moffett (Theta Zeta, 1882) encouraged the Fraternity to take a more progressive approach to expansion. "The founders of the Fraternity were not afraid to break new ground," he explained. "It is by continuing their work,

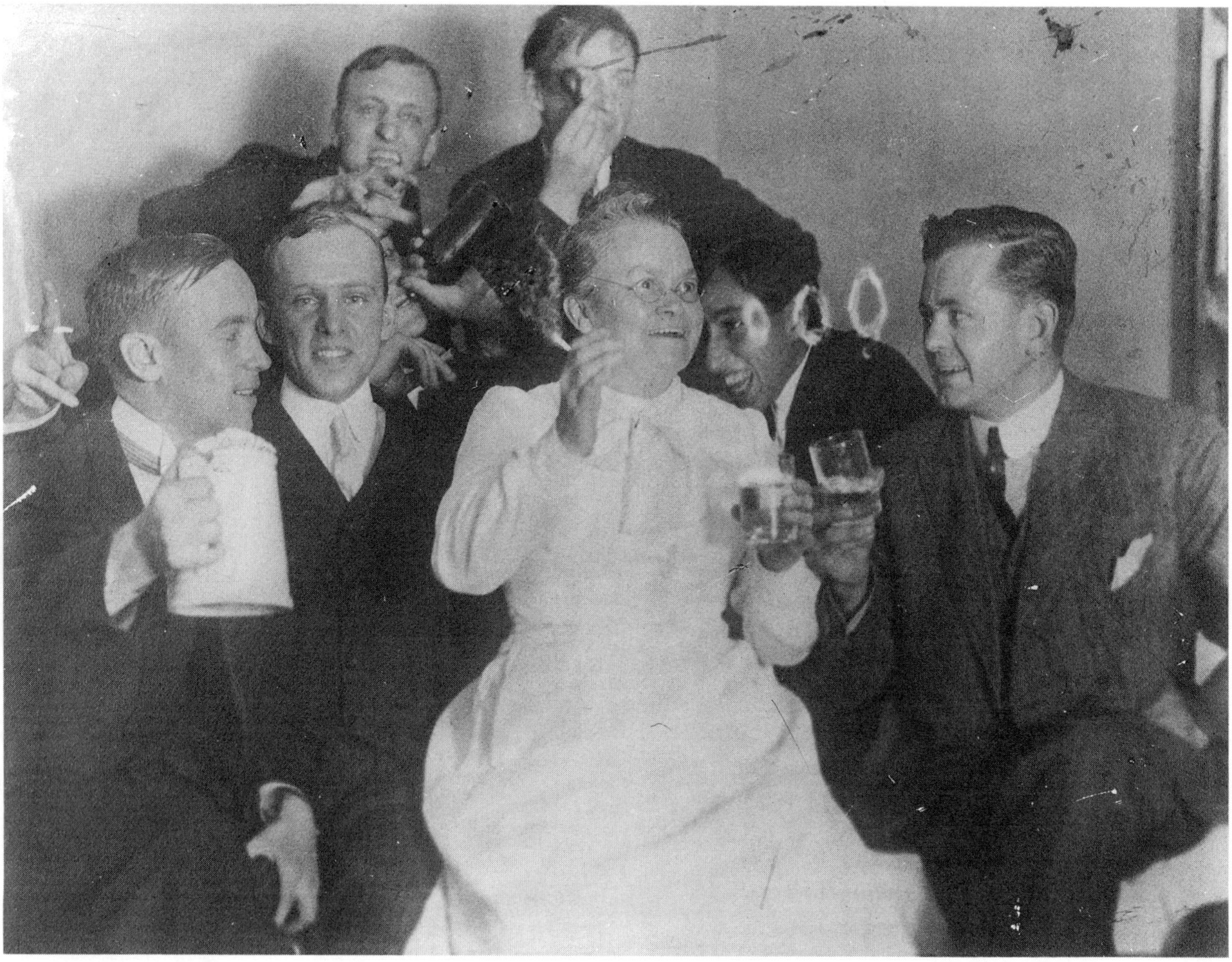

The DKEs set Carrie Nation up for this infamous photo.

not be remaining idly in their beaten tracks, that we shall show ourselves most heedful of their example."

Though the debate would linger for years, the Brotherhood chose to retain its gradual growth policy. In 1898 DKE granted a charter to the University of Toronto in Canada and became an international organization. The new chapter, Alpha Phi, was not the first group outside of the United States to seek a DKE charter. several years earlier a university in England had made an application but the Brotherhood found no outstanding reason to grant it. Alpha Phi was a different story. DKE was suitably impressed with the young men requesting the charter. Almost immediately the fledgling chapter proved the wisdom in DKE's "going international." A well organized group, Alpha Phi members worked diligently to uphold DKE's high standards. Such ambition and upstanding conduct drew the attention of other

PEARY REACHES THE POLE

Another Brother, this time a leader in exploration and scientific research, saw his name go into the pages of history. Robert E. Peary (Theta, 1877) was the first man to reach the North Pole, on April 6, 1909. There, in cold so extreme it froze a flask of brandy he carried under his parka, Peary planted the flags of the United States, Red Cross, Daughters of the American Revolution, Navy League, and Delta Kappa Epsilon.

Peary at the Pole, DKE Flag second from left.

For twenty years Peary had pursued his goal of reaching the North Pole and had braved severe hardship to do it. In 1906 he tried valiantly and came very close, but the trek ended in disappointment. There were times when he and his team doubted they would return alive. After encountering an Arctic blizzard that lasted six days, they knew they would not make their destination, yet pushed on regardless. Though they managed to reach the farthest point north ever documented, their lack of supplies and time forced them to turn back, only to encounter another blizzard. Starvation was close on their heels and disappointment weighed heavily in their hearts.

When Peary and his crew returned home from his 1906 expedition, the New York DKE Association held a dinner in his honor on January 16, 1907. Peary himself gave an account of the adventure. He recalled how he felt when he did not reach the Pole:

> I don't know whether you would call it the uncertainty or the incongruity or the complexity of human nature–but it might be supposed that my feelings at that time of having beaten the record, as it is called, would have been feelings of exultation. As a matter of fact, it was nothing of the kind. . . . I tried to be as thankful as possible that we had beaten the record. . . but the simple fact of beating the record, compared with that on which I had set my heart for years, with that for which I had been straining my life, almost, during the same expedition, fell so far short of that, that my feelings were those of disappointment; and that feeling, combined doubtless, with the physical exhaustion. . . combined to give me the most pronounced case of the blues that I had had during the entire expedition.

His courage and determination did not wane however, and he eventually achieved his goal. Returning to civilization after his successful, historic trek, Peary cabled his wife: "Have made good at last. I have the old Pole." In his telegram announcing his achievement to the Associated Press, the commander requested that information immediately be communicated to DKE. Dekes everywhere cheered in support of the man who dared to follow his dream. In the *DKE Quarterly*, in 1909, John Clair Minot lauded his Brother's accomplishment:

> It is not too much to say that no other world-famous man ever battled with a great problem for a longer time than Peary battled with the inconceivable dangers, hardships, loneliness and despair of those Arctic wastes. With a pluck and a patience that knew no such a possibility as final failure he made defeat the stepping-stone to victory. The annals of our times will be searched in vain for a parallel.

Another dinner was held in Peary's honor on December 18, 1909 at the Hotel Astor. More than six hundred alumni and four hundred undergraduates crowded the hotel ballroom, the world's largest. The hall was decorated with trophies, flags, furs, and other items borrowed from the Museum of Natural History. On the wall opposite the speaker's podium where Peary recounted some of his adventures hung the DKE flag that he had carried with him to the Pole. At the end of the dinner the alumni presented the commander with a huge silver loving cup. It was one of the greatest of Deke Celebrations.

Peary's DKE flag photographed at the Smithsonian Institute.

DKE dinner honoring Commander Peary, December 18, 1909 Hotel Astor, NYC.

student organizations in Canada, and DKE's reputation spread. One year later, DKE established a chapter at McGill University, in Montreal. Alpha Tau's installation on January 12, 1901 was "the most elaborate of any ceremony which had marked the beginning of a new chapter," commented Aldice Warren, in the 1910 *Catalogue of DKE*. Four chapters attended the event, and Alpha Phi sent a delegation of sixteen to serenade and welcome her new sister into the DKE fold.

Meanwhile, the Fraternity expanded when Tau Lambda Chapter was installed at Tulane University, New Orleans, Louisiana, and Delta Kappa was established at the University of Pennsylvania, Philadelphia, Pennsylvania. At the turn of the century membership numbered 14,044 with 850 active members and thirty-eight active chapters.

The Fraternity grew in the West, too, when Sigma Rho was established on the campus of Stanford University in 1902. Two years later saw the birth of Delta Pi chapter at the University of Illinois. In 1906 Rho Delta was installed at the University of Wisconsin in Madison. Despite its cautious approach to granting charters, the Fraternity had made considerable geographic strides.

While new chapters were forming, existing chapters were growing as well. In 1903 Phi changed her membership rule and began recruiting freshmen, thus increasing the number of candidates. Other chapters celebrated grand milestones, such as Upsilon, Alpha Alpha, Iota, and Mu, which celebrated golden anniversaries in the early 1900s. Conventions during those years served as appropriate venues for celebration.

Brother Jimmie Hawes at DKE Club in Paris.
(1918 QUARTERLY, page 190)

In order for the Fraternity to maintain her strength and cohesion as her membership rolls grew, fundamental changes were required. By the end of the decade the massive catalogue published at the dawn of the century desperately needed updating, the Council was too small, and members in remote areas suffered undue expense when traveling to conventions. At DKE's Sixty-second, 1909, Convention, unique because it was held in three different places–it began in New Haven, continued at Hartford, and ended in New York–the Brothers considered imposing a tax upon chapters to raise money for the new catalogue, and employed Aldice Warren as editor. The session leaders also authorized a plan to equalize traveling expenses for all the delegates. With the cost burden more equitably distributed, conventions could expect a larger turnout.

Other changes were made to streamline the Brotherhood's operation. James "Jimmy" Anderson Hawes (Phi, 1894) became the first General Fraternity secretary, the office now known as Executive Director. Shortly after he took office, Hawes began visiting the various chapters, dramatically improving communication between the General Fraternity and active members.

Fraternities Unite

Though DKE was experiencing a boom in popularity with young collegians, anti-fraternity sentiment still ran strong on many college campuses. Fraternities united to stem the opposition. In 1909 DKE became a founding member of the National Interfraternity Council (NIC). The organization was designed to cultivate fraternity growth nationwide and act as an ally in the face of faculty and legislative antagonists. The first meeting was held November 27, 1909 at the University Club in New York, where delegates from twenty-six college fraternities met to consider not only fraternity problems but difficulties affecting the social life of all students on American college campuses. The desired result was to "put these organizations on a broader and stronger basis, with the end in view of making the fraternities a greater power for good in our land." On that day, the NIC vowed to be a voice and platform for fraternity problems and concerns.

DKE's growth was no anomaly. Fraternities across the nation were transforming themselves from "college boy secret societies" to respected organizations that produced leaders, and DKE was rightly proud of her contributions to that goal. To continue producing leaders, the Brotherhood encouraged behavior that promoted excellence among its active members. All chapters were urged to establish and maintain a good library that would include a complete bound set of the *DKE Quarterly,* a set of DKE catalogues and songbooks, and all the local student publications. One reason for such a library was to keep members in the house for both study and recreation, making for stronger relations within the chapter.

"I would not have gotten through college in my chosen profession, which was engineering, if it hadn't been for the support of the guys in my chapter," admitted William Dolan (Phi Epsilon, 1955). "I didn't want to fail in their eyes, so I kept studying and pushing and got through."

Answering the Call

After a notably successful decade, DKE looked forward to the next with great anticipation. Even with its conservative charter-granting philosophy, the Fraternity had experienced major growth, and her success could be measured in other ways as well. By 1910 all but one of the forty-three chapters occupied their own houses. Though Tau Lambda could not make that claim, the chapter worked diligently toward the goal, meeting it the following year.

With a total property value of more than three-quarters of a million dollars, the Fraternity shifted its concentration to overseeing these holdings and the completion of chapter houses. The General Fraternity's headquarters were in New York, but DKE's growth necessitated a branch office. The new office at the Insurance Exchange Building at 29 La Salle Street, Chicago, was set up to handle matters such as ordering pins, catalogues, journals, robes, and other fraternity materials. The branch was also more convenient to members in the Midwest and West.

DKE's prosperity belied the tumultuous times. In 1914 an assassin's bullet set off World War I. War plants turned out newly invented weapons that contributed to the slaughter of more than ten million combatants, and military drafts raised larger armies than ever before. Propaganda whipped up fury and righteousness among many differing factions. World War I involved more countries and caused more destruction than any other war except World War II. Though the United States tried to stay neutral, Americans became outraged by reports of atrocities, such as German submarines sinking unarmed ships.

In the spring of 1917 the United States of America joined the struggle, and Canada followed six months later. Dekes again showed their "true grit." In fact, many Dekes became involved in the war before the rest of America when they volunteered for the Red Cross or joined the armed services of England and France.

In 1918 the *Hartford Courant* printed the following impassioned fraternal cry: "Barbed wire, poison gas, hand-grenades, bayonets–all would be as tissue paper in the face of such an offensive as the Dekes could launch. . . . Bring on your foreign foes! Let them 'put up their dukes.' We'll put up our Dekes!"

Young men who just months before had been busy with collegiate activities found themselves fighting a war on foreign soil. As the number of upperclassmen dwindled in each chapter, the Council called for alumni and remaining actives to "keep the light burning on every altar." General Secretary Hawes called for action on the part of alumni:

> These are times when the old fashioned oratory has passed and nothing now counts but loyal work and results. This is the time when Fraternity leaders, real and nominal, will be weighted in the balance and some probably found wanting. However, the greatest opportunity in our history is now offered for our alumni to show the world what a great college fraternity like Delta Kappa Epsilon can mean to them and can accomplish in its own small corner in the work of the world.

In that time of trial, Dekes took heart in their Fraternity's strengths. Sound and meaningful traditions, well-organized alumni, and an effective centralized government made the Brotherhood a beacon for the members who looked to her for leadership and encouragement in a time of turbulence and confusion. In October 1918 the *DKE Quarterly* printed words of encouragement for those who stayed home:

> If seniors and juniors are few, then let the sophomores not lag behind in assuming responsibility. Happy [is] the chapter where young alumni come back at this season to take hand in things–but if they do not appear on the scene, let not the active members hesitate to call on them.

In that time of trial, Dekes took heart in their Fraternity's strengths.

And above all, in the inevitable zeal for large delegations from the freshman class this fall, let there be no lowering of standards, no sacrifice of quality for the sake of quantity.

General Payton C. March (Rho/Lafayette, 1884), Chief of Staff of the U.S. Forces.

Those Dekes who served in the military distinguished themselves with acts of bravery and meritorious service. Some forty-seven-hundred members were involved in the military of either the United States or its allies during the Great War, more than one-third of DKE's total living membership. Most chapters saw more than 50 percent of their membership in active service. The percentages were even higher for some of the younger chapters.

Both American and Canadian Dekes received military honors and decorations. Brothers who led in the struggle included Payton C. March (Rho, 1884), Chief of Staff of the American Forces, and John Biddle (Omicron, 1880), commanding general of the American army in Great Britain. DeFreest Larner (Gamma Beta, 1920) made a name for himself as a leading American ace, and Charles Kinsolving (Eta, 1916) received the Distinguished Service Cross from General Pershing for his "conspicuous bravery" in one of the first air engagements.

Sadly, Dekes also led in casualties. The first American killed on any front after the United States entered the war was Paul Gannett Osborne (Pi, 1916), who gave his life in the ambulance service. The first man in the U.S. Navy to lose his life was Charles H. Evans (Beta Phi, 1919), and the first American officer to die in the conflict was Louis Jordan (Omega Chi, 1916). In his notable book *Make the Kaiser Dance,* Henry T. Berry (Lambda, 1951) wrote: "At the International Headquarters of Delta Kappa Epsilon there is a bronze plaque containing the names of those brothers who gave their lives in World War I. There are 155 names on the plaque. That is a lot for one small fraternity."

The war also left an impression on those at home. The War Department took over more than five hundred colleges and universities, turning them into temporary training camps, and the students, with the exception of those under eighteen or physically unfit, were inducted into the service. Fraternities throughout the nation suspended nearly all of their activities, and chapter houses were closed down or converted into barracks. The DKE Council encouraged chapters to comply with the requests of the War Department, but to also continue record keeping and house cleaning. The Council recommended each chapter to name a "correspondent" who would update the Council on goings-on.

Beyond the Border

With so many of their Brothers overseas, several chapters suggested DKE establish a meeting place for the Dekes who were serving their country so bravely. The Committee on National Service, jointly appointed by the DKE General Council and Club, devised a plan for an overseas headquarters. A 1918 *DKE Quarterly* explained the committee's reasons for taking such a step:

> If they [Dekes in service] return without the Fraternity having made some effort for its members at this time of crisis, it will certainly be not only a source of just criticism but an indictment from which we should never be relieved. Those remaining at home in comfort must think of our younger members in the other side, and what the Fraternity means to them is shown by the letters being received from our boys "over there."

While DKE tried to work out some arrangements for a club overseas, a group of nearly twenty universities formed the American University Union to offer support to servicemen and DKE was the first fraternity invited to join. Through the union, DKE was able to lease the famous Palais Royale Hotel in the heart of Paris as the Fraternity's headquarters and club. With over two hundred bedrooms and "all the facilities of a first class modern hotel and Club," the establishment offered every comfort to members. Not only could Dekes enjoy some recreation, but medical services were available as well. James Marshall Head (Eta, 1916) was named director of DKE's Overseas Bureau and Club and was offered no pay except expenses. The Fraternity saw it as a labor of love. While her Brothers were defending freedom, DKE would give them all she could, such as encouragement and support.

The club at the Palais Royale Hotel was a success. Dekes were able to meet in a friendly, comfortable environment and exchange ideas and stories amongst themselves, cementing relationships between Brothers and providing relief during a trying time.

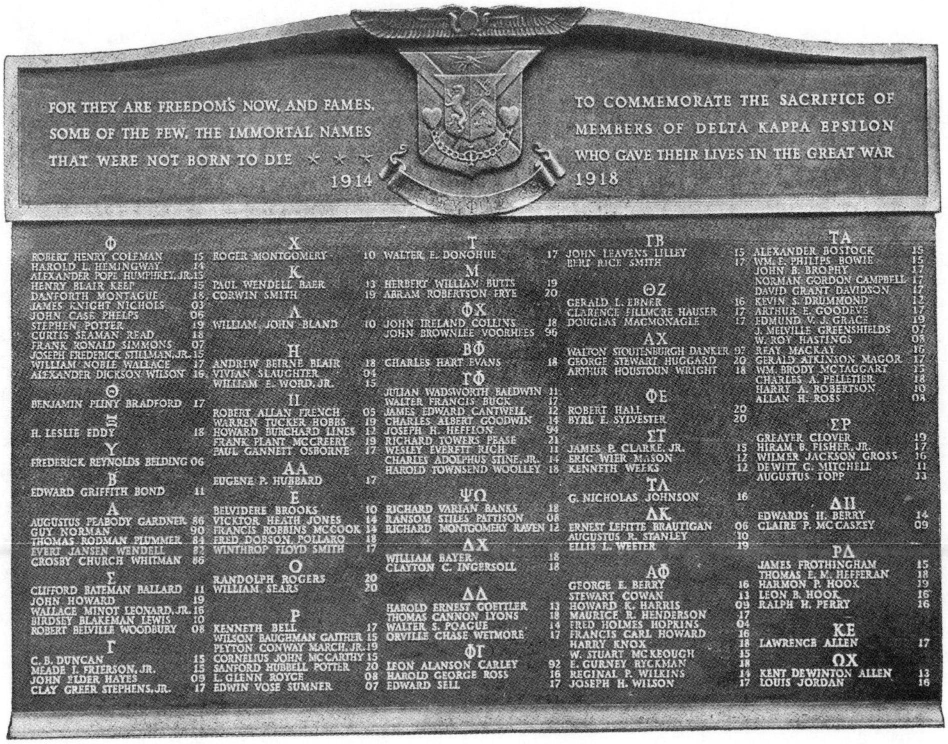

DKE Memorial Tablet at Headquarters.

Diamond Jubilee

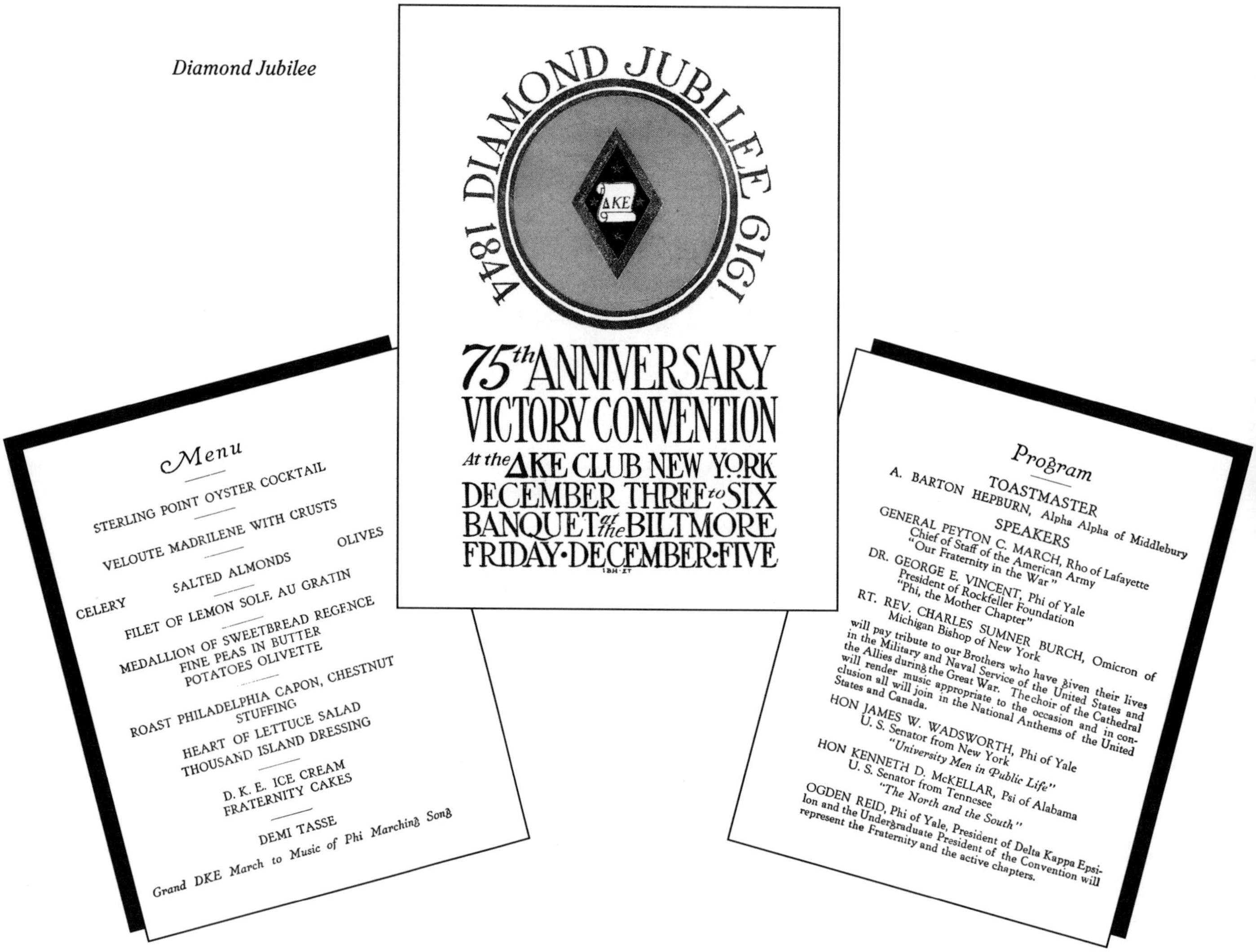

Menu

STERLING POINT OYSTER COCKTAIL

VELOUTE MADRILENE WITH CRUSTS

CELERY SALTED ALMONDS OLIVES

FILET OF LEMON SOLE AU GRATIN

MEDALLION OF SWEETBREAD REGENCE
FINE PEAS IN BUTTER
POTATOES OLIVETTE

ROAST PHILADELPHIA CAPON, CHESTNUT STUFFING

HEART OF LETTUCE SALAD
THOUSAND ISLAND DRESSING

D. K. E. ICE CREAM
FRATERNITY CAKES

DEMI TASSE

Grand DKE March to Music of Phi Marching Song

DIAMOND JUBILEE 1844 1919

75th ANNIVERSARY
VICTORY CONVENTION
At the ΔKE CLUB NEW YORK
DECEMBER THREE to SIX
BANQUET at the BILTMORE
FRIDAY·DECEMBER·FIVE

Program

TOASTMASTER
A. BARTON HEPBURN, Alpha Alpha of Middlebury

SPEAKERS
GENERAL PEYTON C. MARCH, Rho of Lafayette
Chief of Staff of the American Army
"Our Fraternity in the War"
DR. GEORGE E. VINCENT, Phi of Yale
President of Rockfeller Foundation
"Phi, the Mother Chapter"
RT. REV. CHARLES SUMNER BURCH, Omicron of Michigan Bishop of New York
will pay tribute to our Brothers who have given their lives in the Military and Naval Service of the United States and the Allies during the Great War. The choir of the Cathedral will render music appropriate to the occasion and in conclusion all will join in the National Anthems of the United States and Canada.
HON JAMES W. WADSWORTH, Phi of Yale
U. S. Senator from New York
"University Men in Public Life"
HON KENNETH D. McKELLAR, Psi of Alabama
U. S. Senator from Tennesee
"The North and the South"
OGDEN REID, Phi of Yale, President of Delta Kappa Epsilon and the Undergraduate President of the Convention will represent the Fraternity and the active chapters.

In 1918 the Allies won the war, and the United States was ready to move on to a more prosperous future. Delta Kappa Epsilon wanted to do the same. Although relatively small in comparison to many other fraternities, she was still a leader in the fraternity world with forty-three chapters flying her flag and 18,923 men proudly calling themselves Dekes. The Brotherhood had good reason to celebrate. Not only were her members home from war, but she also had seventy-five years of success to commemorate. At DKE's Diamond Jubilee in New York that year, more than three hundred Brothers were present and 99 percent of the undergraduate actives attended. The Brothers rejoiced at the reunion and looked forward to peace and prosperity.

CHAPTER 5

THROUGH THICK AND THIN

The post-war era brought forth a politically conservative climate in the United States, resulting in such measures as the Prohibition Amendment. At the same time, President Woodrow Wilson's attempt to stifle fraternities by abolishing all secret societies at Princeton was a blow to brotherhoods throughout the nation.

Nevertheless, Dekes greeted the "Roaring Twenties" with indomitable enthusiasm. For more than three-quarters of a century their Brotherhood had been a force in the fraternity world, and members could imagine nothing less for her future. Brothers everywhere had seen DKE contribute valiantly to her country, and they knew she could not be swayed by those who tried to silence her. The Fraternity had every intention of showing her spirit, and celebrations for her accomplishments were in order. After the trying times of World War I, the DKE convention committee gave members something to anxiously anticipate: the 1920 convention would be held in Havana, Cuba.

A PARTY IN PARADISE

In 1917 Cuba's president, Mario Garcia Menocal (Delta Chi, 1888), invited the DKE convention to Havana, but plans for the next two conventions had already been made. Finally, in 1919 his gracious invitation was wholeheartedly accepted. The Seventy-sixth Convention would be held "as 1920 went out and 1921 came in" in the "Pearl of the Antilles." Not only did the fraternity world pay close attention to the plans, but so did the general public. For the first time an American fraternity would hold a convention off the continent, and many critics wondered if the reason was to circumvent Prohibition for the festive holiday. One writer reported in a 1921 *DKE Quarterly*:

> Of course a lot of explaining was necessary in the case of some of those suspicious friends who saw, or pretended to see, a case of cause and effect in recent constitution tinkering and a trip of college men to a wet island. It was difficult to convince some of our rivals, whose hearts were overflowing with envy, that we were not of those who now consider the United States as a vast and arid desert bounded on the south by an oasis called Havana and on the north by one called Montreal.

Taking little heed of her critics, DKE leadership worked with President Menocal on the convention plans. On Sunday December 26, 1920, 125 Brothers departed from New York's Pennsylvania Station in a specially chartered DKE train destined for Key West, Florida, picking up other Deke parties at various stops in between. In Georgia, a large group of Dekes from the South and Midwest joined the train after notable festivities in Savannah had been enjoyed by all the Brothers. Two-hundred-fifty Dekes then traveled to Key West, where they boarded the coastal steamer *Governor Cobb* and, after raising the DKE flag on the ship's mast, set off for Cuba.

Shortly after the Dekes arrived, a delegation of fifty Brothers went to the presidential palace to pay respects to Brother Menocal. Because of the president's personal involvement in the

Governor Cobb entering Havana Harbor (QUARTERLY, Vol. 39, #1, page 8).

Convention Banquet at the Vedado Tennis Club, southern end.

convention's organization, the gathering became an event of international interest, and each day English and Spanish newspapers devoted stories on the front pages to the delegates' activities. Dekes were given red-carpet treatment throughout their stay and enjoyed socializing with Havana's elite. Activities included tours of the island, a DKE versus Cuban Athletic Club basketball game, attendance at a jai alai game, gambling, and a memorable New Year's Eve celebration. The convention banquet, held at the Valdado Tennis Club, was the grand finale at which each Deke was given a gift from Cuba's chief executive. John Clair Minot later described the present to Quarterly readers as a beautifully inlaid wooden box containing twenty-five "of the best cigars made in Cuba." The boxes were made specially for the Dekes, and the cover bore the design of the DKE pin, inlaid in woods of different colors.

A Place to Call Home

DKE continued to thrive in the early 1920s. Though her chapter number remained at forty-three, she had fourteen-thousand living members and her property valued nearly one-and-a-half million dollars. In a mere two-year span, ten chapters got new houses.

Omicron at the University of Michigan was one of those chapters. Though the chapter house built in 1888 was one of the most beautiful on campus, Omicron quickly outgrew it. In 1914 the university began a multi-million dollar expansion project and bought several fraternity houses, including Omicron's. It was then that the search for a new home began in earnest. The chapter settled on a residence in Geddes Heights. "Thus far we are the first fraternity in the locality, and believe that we are anticipating the general tendency in this direction," reported the chapter secretary to the General Fraternity. The new location was about a fifteen-minute walk from campus in a newer residential area boasting "generous lawns" and "lacking none of the charm of the older parts of the city."

Securing suitable housing during that time was not always easy.

Securing suitable housing during that time was not always easy. Delta Pi Chapter at the University of Illinois struggled for years to obtain appropriate quarters. After her installation in 1904, the chapter rented a house, and by 1906 they had built a "fairly satisfactory home." There Delta Pi lived until 1921 when the property was sold and the chapter was forced out. In the November 1922 issue of the *DKE Quarterly*, a Delta Pi Brother described the situation:

> This was a serious condition at the time as the housing shortage in Champaign due to the rapid growth of the University, and the high cost of building construction was acute. The chapter was not financially ready to build. . . . The active chapter in the meanwhile had not arranged for housing, and as a result in the fall of 1921 was forced to occupy most inadequate and undesirable quarters. The year of 1921-1922 will go down in the history of the chapter as the practically homeless age.

Finally, the chapter alumni formed a five-member executive board "with full powers to do any and all things to get a house." Three lots were purchased.

Renewing Old Ties

By 1923 DKE had gone twelve years without granting a charter or reviving a chapter, but that ended on April 7 when Zeta Zeta reawakened at Louisiana State University. Originally the chapter had been established at Centenary College, but the Civil War brought an end to the school and the chapter. Since 1908 a group at LSU, "The Friars," many of whom were descendants of the old Zeta Zeta members, had been petitioning the Fraternity for a charter, and twice during that time it had come

Preparing for fhe Future

Despite the increase in property holdings, DKE faced some challenges in the 1920s. Meeting financial obligations became increasingly complicated, and the DKE Holding Company was formed solely for the purpose of holding property title on the club and headquarters. Though the Brotherhood was meeting its expenses, little was left over to cover additional or emergency expenditures. Along with chapter and alumni dues, large revenues were generated from renting space in the DKE Club of New York City for various functions, but the interest on the property's mortgages and carrying charges absorbed almost all of it. By the early 1920s the need for renovation at the Club was becoming obvious and the organization had few funds to spare. Dekes were asked to contribute whatever they could for the project, and the Brothers responded with zeal. Yet the whole process had revealed a weakness in the organization, and DKE wanted to address it before any other financial difficulty arose. Richard T. Greene (Phi Chi, 1889) had an idea that would secure DKE's financial situation:

> Additional revenue should be obtained through the creation of a permanent endowment fund, which can be raised only by voluntary contributions of individual Dekes who realize the dignity and importance of their Fraternity, the worth of its works and the necessity of placing it upon a permanent foundation.

And so the endowment fund project was born. The goal was to secure one million dollars for the fund without "engaging in a high pressure campaign." For several years efforts were made to establish the trust, but all met with failure until a plan was accepted by the Council in October 1931. The plan would contribute part of the existing alumni dues to the fund and enlarge the *DKE Quarterly's* circulation. The *Quarterly's* own subscription endowment fund became the "nucleus" of the General Endowment Trust Fund of Delta Kappa Epsilon. The endowment was set up in such a way that funds donated would remain in the trust and only the interest could be spent for the Fraternity or the various chapters. Dekes could contribute to the permanent fund and at the same time reap personal benefits, such as a reduction on annual dues and a lifetime subscription to the *Quarterly*, depending on the amount donated. Overseeing the trust was the responsibility of four trustees: the chairman of the endowment committee, the treasurer of the Council, the editor of the *Quarterly*, and one other Brother to be chosen by the Council.

within one vote of being accepted. In the meantime, the Friars, a prosperous group who owned its own home and had enough funds to build one "twice as commodious and comfortable," had been invited to join several other prestigious national fraternities, but their hearts were set on DKE. Finally, in 1922 the petition was unanimously recommended by the Council and easily passed the Convention. The Friars adopted a motto that translated from Greek means "Devotion is rewarded."

In 1928 another chapter with deep DKE roots, Chi at the University of Mississippi, was revived. Reissuing Chi's charter had been debated for several years, and at the 1927 convention no dissenting votes were cast, the first unanimous convention decision since 1876. There was no great mystery as to why Chi garnered such support. Her history was as rich and honorable as the Fraternity herself. Chi was the first Greek-letter society at the university and the eighth DKE chapter. Still, Chi had become inactive twice. The first time was in 1861 when almost all of her Brothers joined the Confederate army. They rolled up the charter, placed it in a lead container, and buried it. One hundred

"Before this act went into effect, DKE... gracefully withdrew."

Chi Dekes donned gray uniforms and became part of the "Eleventh Mississippi." Of the 135 men in that company, only twenty-four could be accounted for at the end of the war. Only three Chi Brothers survived, but their loyalty to DKE was undiminished. In 1866 they dug up the priceless charter and struggled to reestablish their beloved chapter.

The second time Chi closed was the result of a strong movement in the state against fraternities which cited their exclusivity as the main criticism. In 1912 all such organizations were legally barred from institutions "maintained in whole or in part at the expense of the state." In December 1930 the *DKE Quarterly* described Chi's dignity in those troubling times: "Before this act went into effect, DKE and perhaps some others gracefully withdrew. The Dekes' original charter and metal container were surrendered to their National Council before it was called for."

Finally, after a long and frustrating battle in the legislature, the antifraternity law was repealed in the late 1920s. Profraternity activists argued that many of the nation's great men were members of Greek letter societies. One Chi Brother explained the Mississippi Legislature's change of heart:

> Few Mississippians will lift a hand against any banner that is borne by Thomas Jefferson, Jefferson Davis, L.Q.C. Lamar, Stonewall Jackson, and Robert E. Lee. Confronted by such an array of knighthood, the "anti-frats" began to wobble, to desert, to stampede: so that the final vote stood seventy "yeas" to forty-nine "nays." As a result of which, DKE and other fraternities marched back triumphantly to their ancient camp at "Ole Miss."

Beginning New Traditions

In spite of strong opposition, fraternities flourished and antifraternity sentiments subsided somewhat in the late 1920s. DKE's guarded, extreme secrecy gave way to more open operations as her beneficial work, wealth, and influence became widely known. Society in general and college faculties in particular began to recognize the contributions DKE and other fraternities made to higher education and to the nation. The Brotherhood had an honorable record of service, and it could no longer be ignored. Though fraternities still had to contend with nay-sayers, a general air of acceptance began to emerge. This new, open sentiment fostered goodwill among chapters and their communities, resulting in the adoption of two new customs: Guest Night and Chapter Night.

Guest Night included an evening meal or Sunday brunch each week to which a number of people were invited. Chapters exercised discretion in their choices, hosting people of different professions and interests, such as faculty of universities and colleges, members of other fraternities, alumni, nonfraternity men, and townspeople. The visitors were entertained after the meal, but the festivities were not allowed to interfere with regular study hours. The practice promoted feelings of camaraderie between fraternity men, nonfraternity men, and faculty. Many guests returned the invitation, so Dekes experienced other fraternities and met the families of faculty. Such occasions taught DKE members how to act in social situations, thus training them for rush season, not to mention later life.

Chapter Nights, occurring about once a month, were evenings devoted to reports and debates amongst Brothers and occasional talks by visitors.

The effort to bring chapter members closer to their communities was a great success, and alumni began to recognize a marked change in the behavior of the actives. Their public manner grew more subdued, and they were better dressed and "generally more attractive to strangers." Alumni were surprised at how these young men seemed so worldly-wise and businesslike, with less "boyish enthusiasm," personal characteristics that earned public respect for the organization, and fraternities as a whole.

"...it was the best fraternity in the country..."

William "Hut" Hutton (Sigma Rho, 1926)

UNITY IN HARDSHIP

By 1926 Delta Kappa Epsilon had forty-five active chapters. William "Hut" Hutton (Sigma Rho, 1926), remembers the Fraternity's success in the mid-twenties. He said he joined DKE because "it was the best fraternity in the country," and he insists that it helped groom him for the challenges of being a captain in the U.S. Navy and later a successful stockbroker on Wall Street. Adolph Billet (Tau Lambda, 1935) also remembered the pre-depression prosperity. "You could take a date to the biggest movie in town, stop on the way home and get a Coca-Cola, and still have twenty-five cents left out of a dollar!" he exclaimed.

The heyday of the mid-1920s did not last. In 1929 the stock market crash sent shock waves throughout the country, throwing the United States into its worst economic depression. Members of the Fraternity were no less affected than the rest of the country. Paul Gauger (Zeta Zeta, 1934) recalls the hardships he faced: "I had to sell odds and ends in my senior year to finish school."

Yet the Brotherhood tried to rise above the economic challenges by focusing on the future. Never diverted from her main purpose of helping young men become leaders, DKE was able to instill hope in members while the nation wallowed in despair. Whitelaw Reid (Phi, 1933) still recalls why he joined the Brotherhood during those trying times: "DKE was considered one of the top fraternities at the time. It was an honor to be picked for it."

By holding true to its principles and building together, Delta Kappa Epsilon was able to maintain all of its forty-five active chapters, and in fact, numerous chapters celebrated milestone anniversaries, such as Alpha Chi's Golden Jubilee. Two new chapters were installed, as well: Theta Rho at the University of California at Los Angeles in 1932, followed by another Canadian chapter, Delta Phi, at the University of Alberta at Edmonton.

Along with other international fraternities, DKE recognized the benefits of unity in an otherwise disheartening age. In his annual report to the eighteenth Interfraternity Conference held in New York at the end of the decade, conference chairman Henry R. Johnston (Epsilon, 1909) reviewed the work of his administration, paying particular attention to the spiritual side of fraternity life, alumni, and scholastic activities. His report concluded:

> We are confident that the interfraternity movement, the foundations of which were so firmly laid seventeen years ago, will continue to grow and expand in such fashion that the fraternities will more and more do their part with the colleges and universities of the country in turning out as citizens of the United States men of high capacity, lofty ideals and devoted patriotism.

"Dues in the early thirties were thirty-two dollars a month..."

Amedee Wade Noland (Zeta Zeta, 1936)

As the depression wore on, Fraternity members continued to grapple with the economic concerns that shadowed much of their lives as well as their beloved organization. Fraternities across the nation lost members who simply could not afford to pay the dues. Still, DKE was so important to many of her members that they endured hardship in order to meet their obligation. "Dues in the early thirties were thirty-two dollars a month," said Amedee Wade Noland (Zeta Zeta, 1936). "My father had a little brown bag of twenty-five-cent pieces from his country store. That's what paid my dues."

In the mid-thirties the federal government, headed by Franklin Delano Roosevelt, began taking measures to ease the suffering. The New Deal was enacted, and Americans concerned themselves with the welfare of their fellowman. The mainstream citizenry had learned harsh lessons about economic insecurity and a deeper sense of compassion spread through the country.

That compassion, however, did not warm the hearts of fraternities' adamant opposition, and once again members of secret societies were forced to battle the ever-present, loud minority of antifraternity liberals. So prevalent was the problem that in 1936, 108 undergraduate representatives of the nation's fraternities met with 263 educators and fraternity leaders at the National Interfraternity Conference. The delegates were led by H. Maurice Darling Alpha Phi, 1903, a former president of DKE and a graduate of the University of Toronto.

Fraternity members were encouraged to promote high academic standards...

The conference focused on the criticism fraternities were receiving nationwide. Alumni and leaders reminded the delegates that the very existence of fraternities was tied to the well-being of the institutions. Fraternity members were encouraged to promote high academic standards and cooperation between college and fraternity.

Delta Kappa Epsilon was ready to do her part. In 1937 Dekes at Hamilton College were instrumental in starting a new gymnasium fund for the school by initiating Cereal Day. Instead of eating their usual fare on Friday nights, the students ate cereal, drank a glass of milk, and gave the forty-cent difference between the cost of the simple meal and the usual dinner to the gym fund. The chapter estimated its members' weekly donation would be approximately fifteen dollars, and when all the other fraternities on campus joined the drive the amount would jump to 150 dollars. Other money-saving ideas were implemented as well, to the eventual benefit of the college and the Hamilton fraternity world.

Critics were not interested, however, in the efforts DKE and other fraternities were making or had made in the past. In 1938 concern escalated within fraternities resulting in another national meeting in New York. Delegates of practically every national fraternity attended, including one hundred undergraduates representing seventy colleges and universities. Yet a spirit of cooperation was evidenced by the attendance of approximately fifty presidents of educational institutions and deans of men. These leaders encouraged fraternities to establish international scholarships for exchange students, develop programs toward better fraternity conditions, report progress toward developing "social mindedness," and improve relationships with civic and college communities.

Dr. Ernest Martin Hopkins (Pi 1901), President Dartmouth College

Though DKE strongly battled the unfair and unjustified attacks on fraternities in general, she never faltered in her focus on members. She was polishing some for greatness and rewarding others for loyalty, and the wars she fought were further lessons for her members to stand by their convictions. So as the Fraternity defended itself and others like it, chapters continued to celebrate anniversaries and forge lifelong friendships and loyalty. Indeed, there was nowhere to go but forward.

CHAPTER 6

OF BROTHERS AND BRAVERY

As the battle between antifraternity proponents and Brothers waged on, the United States also became embroiled in war in the early 1940s. World War II began in 1939 in Europe when Adolph Hitler's German "war machine" invaded Poland and went on to crush Denmark, Luxembourg, the Netherlands, Belgium, Norway, and France. Soon, Great Britain stood alone against Hitler. The United States actively participated in multinational talks but was hesitant to become involved. She was jolted out of her ambivalence, however, by a swift and brutal attack from an Asian aggressor on December 7, 1941.

FOR LIBERTY AND JUSTICE

An alliance of treachery was formed between Germany, Italy, and Japan, but the Axis forces would later regret their invasions of the Soviet Union and the South Pacific, bringing two powerful nations into the struggle against them. After Japanese forces attacked military bases at Pearl Harbor, the United States could no longer sit on the sidelines. Lieutenant William G. Caffey Jr. (Psi, 1941) was near Pearl Harbor when it was attacked and later described the experience in a letter to his father:

> I was lying in bed on the said morning of December 7, 1941, reading the paper—having been up for about an hour—when I was shocked out of the funnies by a terrific explosion. . . .only seconds later, another and another explosion shook the house. Then I knew that it was the

The Ringing of the Crouse Chimes

Though it was a difficult time throughout "Dekedom," the "flickering flame" at DKE altars was kept alight. Other traditions were diligently observed as well. The ringing of the Crouse Chimes at Syracuse University is but one example.

In the late 1800s D. Edgar Crouse gave the chimes to the university and entrusted their ringing to his friend C. Winfred Douglas (Phi Gamma, 1891), who later became Canon Douglas, a priest of the Episcopal Church and the leading authority on hymnology in the country. From then on, Phi Gamma Dekes continued the tradition of ringing the chimes. When the chapter closed for World War II, the chimemaster trained four Alpha Phi sorority sisters and handed the tradition over to them until the end of the war. "The Alpha Phis executed their trust in the most exemplary manner until the spring of 1946 when they returned the responsibility to the Dekes upon their resumption of active fraternity life on campus," W. Dexter Wilson (Phi Gamma, 1912) reported in the December 1946 *DKE Quarterly*.

real thing. . . we all started dressing as quickly as possible. By this time the bombs were crashing on both sides of us, and the smoke and dust from P.H. and Hickam nearly cut off the light of the sun. Both the planes and ground machine guns were going full blast, and with the roar of the plane motors and the explosion of the bombs you can imagine how much noise there was. . . .As I looked out of the window while dressing, I saw one plane dive low over the house and could clearly see the big red rising sun on the plane's fuselage. . .

Life throughout the United States changed after that attack. No longer was the country safe from the aggression that had plagued the Old World for the previous two years. No longer could Americans take for granted their safety; distance from Europe and Asia would no longer protect them. "After Pearl Harbor, we had the searchlights up in front of the fraternity house looking for the planes," recalled Doug Laidlaw (Theta Rho, 1943). "Everybody thought the Japanese were going to land at any time. We had blackouts and brownouts every night. Fraternity life was built around that."

Just as they had done three other times in the past, Dekes rallied to protect democracy and their countries. Young men who only a year before had voiced their scorn for war had a change of heart and were some of the first to sign up. A Phi Gamma Chapter member noted, "The carefree college atmosphere gave way to the sober realization that in the very near future the campus would be superseded by military training camps, textbooks by weapons of war."

By mid-1944 more than six thousand Dekes were in active duty in all branches of service, and those remaining at home supported the war effort in any way they could. Chapters' sizes dwindled, but the Council resolved that as long as there was one Deke at a chapter, it would be considered active. If a chapter became inactive, the Council requested that alumni assure the proper closure and storage of chapter records and possessions. Many chapter houses were given over to the universities, which rented them to service groups.

Honor During Adversity

The times were demoralizing, but the alumni and youth of DKE who remained at home did not forget to celebrate DKE's accomplishments in spite of the upheaval the world faced. Milestones were reached and duly honored, albeit quietly. On

November 17, 1943, Beta Chi observed seventy-five years of DKE brotherhood. Though many of her members were fighting in the war, they did not forget the auspicious occasion, and nearly one hundred servicemen sent congratulatory letters filled with their best wishes and warmest regards. The chapter had closed, but the sixty-three alumni who attended the dinner pledged their support for Beta Chi and vowed to do everything possible to reestablish it at the end of World War II. Even the devastating current events did not quell the enthusiasm of these loyal alumni. Dick Gottron (Beta Chi) wrote the following in his letter urging support for the occasion:

> On November 17, 1868, our chapter was granted its charter. . . .Since then more than five hundred aspiring neophytes have achieved the coveted diamond pin to form a continuous chain of brotherhood through half a score of Houses on two campuses, surviving booms and depressions, the wars and peace, the heartaches and happiness of seventy-five eventful years. The mind's eye of each of us recalls the dances, football games, rushing parties, intramurals, the comradeship, and the thousand-and-one interests which went into our own short span of active life–and these hundreds of individual impressions unite to form a giant kaleidoscopic pattern of Beta Chi through three-quarters of a century of cultured contribution to the good life of America.

Of the Dekes who served, more than three hundred did not return...

Gamma Phi at Wesleyan University was another chapter that turned seventy-five in the spring of 1942. It also had the pleasure of burning the $45,000 mortgage on its handsome graystone chapter house at the same time. Approximately 150 alumni and chapter members celebrated the dual observance. Her sister in history, Phi Gamma, turned seventy-five a few years later, after the war finally ended. Both chapters had been affiliated with a group known as the "Mystic Seven" before DKE had chartered them.

Healing the Wounds

When World War II finally ended in 1945, the losses were devastating. More people had been killed than any other war in history. Of the Dekes who served, more than three hundred did not return and forty-six chapters lost members. Rutgers and Middlebury suffered the most, each losing fourteen men, with Mu close behind. "We have a plaque in the house with the names of ten men we lost in World War II, and I knew six of them," said Joe DeBragga (Mu, 1943). "I think of that often."

The war affected fraternities in other ways as well, and DKE began to see a new kind of member. Men who had known firsthand the terrors of war returned to the United States with serious educational goals. At the University of Minnesota, for example, veterans outnumbered nonveterans in the fraternities, with DKE having the highest percentage. These men were older and wiser than the students of the past, and many were married with families of their own. With a more mature outlook and a strengthened sense of values, veterans contributed a great deal to DKE's chapters by providing firm guidance to the youthful members and a sense of responsibility to their Brotherhood. "When I went to Colgate, more than half the students were veterans," remembered John R. Wilson (Mu, 1952). "They had been through hell and back and they wanted to get an education. Most important, they brought direction to the Fraternity."

Moving Forward, Looking Back

William W. "Dutch" Elder (Epsilon, 1908).

The strength and integrity of the veterans was one more asset to the Fraternity's legacy of honor. DKE had survived four wars, and she had not lost any property during the last one. She had forty-seven active and eleven inactive chapters, and her living membership numbered approximately twenty-two thousand. Only four chapters–Alberta, UCLA, Manitoba, and Kenyon–did not have houses. Still, DKE had not held its annual convention since the war started, and during that time she had turned one hundred. As soon as World War II ended, preparations for the celebration began, culminating in the 1947 Centennial Convention.

Though the night of December 26th brought 25.8 inches of snow, conventioneers prevailed. The lights in the Council Office at 50 Vanderbilt Avenue and at the Biltmore helped guide in all Dekes who had braved the storm. Fraternity Field Secretary William W. "Dutch" Elder (Epsilon, 1908) began to wonder if the convention would be reduced to "a cozy little tea party of the few hardy souls who are usually catalogued as 'early arrivals,'" but the next morning phones were busily ringing while staff reassured Dekes that the convention would go on as planned.

Delegates, alternates and alumni trickled in for registration, swapping stories their travels. One group even took shelter in a warm jail. It may have slowed Brothers' arrivals, but the weather failed to hamper the event. Members excitedly greeted

Lt. General Price J. Montague (Alpha Phi, 1904), DKE's Highest Ranking Officer in World War II.

each other and celebrated the longevity of DKE. Secretary Elder warmly greeted the delegation:

> We are meeting here to celebrate the Centennial of our founding–a celebration made late by war. We have reason to rejoice in our complete recovery from the blows dealt by this war, and we have reason to be proud of the fraternity and of its members. Delta Kappa Epsilon has prospered in fat years and surmounted the difficulties of lean ones, and has maintained leadership for over one hundred years. We have already entered our second century and I know that it is not only your desire but your determination that our Fraternity shall continue to maintain leadership, continue to produce useful citizens and continue to prosper.

Conviviality was not the only function of the convention, however. After conducting necessary business, the delegation moved to Connecticut to honor the slain Dekes of World War II. The service was held at Yale University's Dwight Chapel with a tribute by Hon. Justice Price J. Montague (Alpha Phi, 1904) [Justice Montague as a Lt. General, was DKE's highest ranking officer in World War II. He was a founder of Alpha Tau, Manitoba, and later was Honorary President of DKE and Justice of the Manitoba Court of Appeals.]

And so the Brotherhood bid farewell to a century of achievements and sorrows...

> On this Sabbath Day here where our Fraternity was founded over 100 years ago, we have come from all over our two countries to honor those 300 of our brothers who at sea, on land, or in the air, fell in the struggle or in preparation for it. They gave up all that was dear to them in order that the democratic way of life should continue and civilization survive. . . . Wherever their resting places may be, including those known only to God, we here today will remember them, and the red blood they poured out will sanctify and keep alive the altar fires of their chapters.

Justice Kenneth C. Royall (Beta, 1914) also eulogized those who fought and gave the supreme sacrifice. In times of trouble or strife, he said, Brothers should remember those who gave their lives to protect their countries. The service concluded as the organist played "We Hail Thee Holy Goddess" while the assembled Dekes stood in silence and reflected on the words of the DKE Roll of Honor:

> Not for Fame or Reward, not for Place or for Rank, not allured by Ambition or goaded by Necessity, but in simple Obedience to Duty as they understood it, these men suffered all sacrificed all, dared all—and Died.

And so the Brotherhood bid farewell to a century of achievements and sorrows, prosperity and struggles, peace and war. She was weary of battle and hopeful for better times to come. Proud of her long, reputable history, she looked forward with confidence as a new era dawned. One good omen was the installation of two new chapters: Delta Epsilon at Northwestern University, and Lambda Delta at Southern Methodist University.

Among those who returned from battle was Bill Henderson, (Zeta Zeta, 1939) who, after combat duty as an officer on New Caledonia and Saipan, was on his way to the final assault on the Japanese mainland when the war ended. Bill came to New York and began a more than three decade career with DKE. It had been decided to provide Dutch Elder with an assistant and Bill was recruited for the job. Only a few Deke chapters remained active during the war, and Bill and Dutch had their hands full reactivating the Fraternity. The change to peacetime status, with its tremendous influx of veterans on the G.I. Bill, kept Bill on the road for months at a time. After serving under Dutch Elder, Bill would be appointed Executive Director and serve for more than 20 years. In 1945 Bill was asked to edit the *Deke Quarterly* for just two issues, until a permanent editor could be found. Nine years and 36 issues later, he was still at it. The permanent editor,

William M. Henderson (Zeta Zeta, 1939) at old DKE Headquarters at the Yale Club.

John E. Bierck, (Alpha Chi, 1917) arrived in 1954 and, on his death in 1962 was succeeded by T. Harold Forbes, Jr. (Mu, 1935) of the *New York News*. In 1969, Bill again was named editor to serve until his retirement in 1973.

The new path DKE traveled was a continuation of her past, and this was especially clear as many stalwart chapters also turned one hundred years old. Gamma at Vanderbilt and Psi at the University of Alabama turned one hundred in 1947, with Chi and Upsilon Chapters following close behind in 1950. Only five years later, five more chapters, Eta, Iota, Pi, Lambda, and Omicron, all reached that milestone. Meanwhile, Alpha Phi, Delta Kappa, Tau Lambda, and Tau Alpha celebrated semi-centennials and Alpha Chi turned seventy-five. For all, such anniversaries gave pause for reflection and contemplation. Members and alumni looked back on DKE's history and vowed to be as great in the future as their predecessors had been in the past.

Κηρόθεν Φίλοι ἀεί

Courage in an Inferno

During those years of celebration and commemoration, tragedy struck one DKE chapter. At nearly 4 a.m. on February 27, 1949, Kenyon College's oldest and largest dormitory, "Old Kenyon," burned to the ground. The remains smoldered for more than twenty days. Since fraternities on that campus were not allowed chapter houses, Lambda lost its ninety-five year-old home which had been located in Old Kenyon.

The fire not only destroyed the massive structure, but also brought injury and death to students who moments before had been sleeping peacefully. Eight men died, twelve were hospitalized, and countless others were treated for minor injuries and shock.

During the emergency, Lambda Brothers demonstrated leadership and bravery. They called two fire departments and the state troopers and roused the other residents of the West Wing. Two Brothers braved the smoke-filled fourth floor to make sure no one was trapped there. After making sure all the students were out, they tried to save whatever they could. Then there was nothing left to do but watch their home burn. The chapter members wrote the following in a letter to their alumni two days later:

By this time flames filled all the rooms of Middle Kenyon. We watched the Wing carefully, hoping that the fire wall between West Division and West Wing would hold. But suddenly there came a great flash in the Bulls-eye [circular window on the fourth floor of West Wing], and then we knew it was all over. The Bulls-eye burned hard, and intermittently new flashes of flame appeared in the other darkened rooms until the whole wing was nothing but a shell of flame.

Two hours later nothing was left "but the walls and burning rubble."

Old Kenyon Burns—February 27, 1949.

CHAPTER 7

SETTING A STANDARD

The 1950s brought some peace of mind to Dekes. Turmoil still beset the world as the United States and Soviet Union flexed their muscles, yet North American fraternities saw tremendous growth. Members were filled with hope and enthusiasm for their countries as well as their Fraternity, regardless of the "Communist threat" and military involvement in Korea. Hamilton "Ham" Richardson (Tau Lambda, 1955), America's top-ranked tennis player in 1956 and 1958, remembered the upbeat attitude prevalent during his undergraduate years. "We felt we were lucky to be who and where we were. We liked ourselves, and we loved our country," he recalled in a 1993 interview. "We thought America was the greatest."

Jim McCarthy (Phi, 1956) agreed. "There were no worries," he said. "We had just won a world war. The country was in wonderful shape, and everyone was happy and optimistic."

The Fraternity, too, was optimistic. E. Jansen Hunt (Upsilon, 1925), who had been vice-president of DKE for three years, was elected president in 1950. In accepting the post, Hunt told the Council that the Brotherhood "must continue aggressively to demonstrate the tremendous value of the whole college fraternity system by teaching honor, responsibility, and leadership. We're devoting our time to something that's alive and that will grow bigger and better." To prove his point, the Fraternity needed only to look at the number of chapters celebrating noteworthy anniversaries. During that decade alone, eleven chapters turned one hundred, several others reached the half-century mark, and one became seventy-five.

BETTERING THE BROTHERHOOD

By 1948 most chapters were operating well...

Despite all her celebrations, the Fraternity faced some important issues. Military mobilization in Korea resulted in fluctuating enrollment in colleges and universities, and DKE wanted to be prepared in case chapter sizes dwindled again. In addition, Post-World War II chapter houses had been crowded due to zealous initiating. By bolstering numbers, many chapters reasoned, the health of the Fraternity as a whole was ensured.

Fortunately, the military struggle in Korea was less of a concern for DKE than other wars because the United States government changed its method of calling young men to service. At the 106th DKE Convention in 1950, Colonel R.P. Johnson Jr. (Zeta Zeta) clarified the new policy to young Dekes. Though they needed to register for the draft, he explained, enlisting was not encouraged. Furthermore, all students would be exempted from induction until they finished school.

This was good news for the Fraternity. Finally, members could focus on improving the Brotherhood in areas that had been neglected during the upheaval of the 1930s and early 1940s. By 1948 most chapters were operating well, but a few were experiencing such problems as poor financial management. Some actives were not paying their dues and other bills promptly, leaving their Brothers to carry the burden. Meanwhile, the costs of running the chapters were increasing. The Council suggested that alumni review chapter expenses and help enforce rules regarding prompt payment. "Every chapter should be self-supporting, and every member of the chapter should feel it incumbent upon himself to bear his share of the load," Fraternity Secretary Dutch Elder told his fellow Dekes at the convention in 1948.

Serious problems were cropping up in other areas as well. That same year Fraternity alumni were chagrined to learn the results of the National Interfraternity Conferences report on scholarship, which revealed DKE chapters were lagging behind other fraternities. Elder encouraged chapters to focus more on academics and less on having a good time. "I know, and I think you know, that the cause of this low scholarship is due to extracurricular inactivity or to such activity as is not recognized in the Year Book," he admonished. He encouraged all Brothers, alumni and actives alike, to meet the challenge. "Delta Kappa Epsilon has survived several major conflicts and withstood several periods of depression," he reminded them. "Trouble always brings friends closer together, as true friendship helps in bearing burdens."

Accordingly, scholarship became a focus of the 1950s. The Fraternity began addressing academic problems through a multi-faceted approach, reasoning that scholarship would improve if unity and pride were encouraged. In an all-out effort to make the Brotherhood the best it could be, DKE sought to improve its standing in academics, finance, and community and university relations. Her goal was for each chapter to become the most prestigious group on campus, and her efforts to reach it were intense.

Wisdom in Youth

One avenue the Fraternity took to unite and strengthen her chapters was through the Deke Conference Camps. These annual week-long undergraduate retreats in the Adirondacks near Lake Placid, New York, had begun as early as August 1938 as a Council experiment to create solidarity among chapters through recreation and round-table discussions. The camps were suspended during the war, but in the late forties they resumed with gusto, and the Adirondacks became their traditional home.

DKE Adirondack Camp (far left, "Dutch" Elder; seated, Bill Henderson; standing, Dick Clark).

Hazing

Scholarship was not the only topic of conversation at the 1959 conference camp. Hazing was another matter that had grave implications for the Fraternity, and the issue was hotly debated among the undergraduates that year. Every one of the sixteen chapters represented by one or more undergraduates favored limitations, if not exclusion, of hazing during pledgeship. Some Brothers suggested that hazing be replaced by community service projects and other endeavors that would benefit both the pledges and their chapters. Others contended that hazing had a "place" in fraternity life. Though there were arguments in favor of the practice, the Fraternity had dealt with the consequences of the negative publicity as early as 1905 when a young pledge died on some railroad tracks near Kenyon College. Though an investigation later determined that the youth had fallen asleep on the tracks while waiting for others to meet him, public sentiment immediately swung against DKE, and rumors flew that the boy had been tied to the tracks as a piece of hazing.

In a number of chapters, however, the practice of hazing had become traditional, however, and despite the International Fraternity's discouragement, it continued. Some instances were mild. Hugh Thistlethwaite (Zeta Zeta, 1937) still remembers what he had to do as a pledge. "I had to crawl around the living room while the frat members paddled me when I went by," he said in a 1993 interview.

Other Brothers took pledges without money miles from the chapter house and let them try to find their way back home. On one occasion the pledges were lucky enough to see a lighted house. Thistlethwaite was there and vividly remembers the prank. He said the resident listened to the plight of the pledges and offered to take the boys home, for a price. Luckily, one of the youths had hidden money in his clothes. "As I recall," Thistlethaite mused, "we beat some of the chapter members back to the Deke house."

Yet the acceptability of hazing dramatically declined after World War II. Veterans who joined DKE had witnessed too much in the war to condone behavior designed to humiliate young men. Their attitude spread, and before long most chapters curtailed the practice.

Hazing did not completely disappear, however, and to offset any problems arising from such conduct, the 1959 Deke Conference Camp supported the convention's recommendation to empower the Council to discipline chapters or individuals whose actions could be detrimental to DKE.

In his 1959 Convention address, Dr. John R. Hubbard (Omega Chi, 1938) lauded the conference camp's efforts to modify the practice and had some suggestions of his own. "I wonder if anyone has ever thought of intellectual hazing?" he asked. "What about a pledge class being instructed to engage a tutor and learn Russian? After all, as Greeks we are supposed to be concerned with a language other than our own. . . . It would certainly be less stupid and less wasteful of time than many things I was made to do, and, in my turn, made others do."

Hazing incidents in recent years have tended to be harmless though memorable. Conway Farrell (Zeta Zeta, 1970) still recalls shaving his head and wearing a beanie, among other things. "I had to talk to Mike the Tiger [the Louisiana State University mascot] every morning for five days and I was also required to attend the first football game of the year wearing pajamas."

In DKE today, even these mild antics are regarded as unnecessary, and if not actually physically harmful to the individual, they are potentially fatal to a chapter at the growing number of campuses where "hazing" of any nature is grounds for chapter expulsion. The Fraternity Board of Directors has stated unequivocally that "No chapter shall conduct hazing activities." Fun though (to some) hazing might have been, it's day in DKE is over.

The camps were praised by the undergraduates who attended them. Though some were reluctant to attend when first chosen, they soon learned that the experience was valuable and enjoyable. A great deal of time and effort went into the discussions, but there was also plenty of time for recreation and new friends.

The camps trained active members for leadership through a balance of fun and brainstorming. "One cannot emphasize enough the value of this cross-exchange of ideas, which in each of our minds gave rise to a new idea or solution to a problem that somewhere existed in our own chapters," wrote Charles K. Koones (Epsilon, 1954) in a December 1951 *Deke Quarterly* article.

Aside from chapter management, subject matter often centered on ways to improve scholarship within each chapter. By the end of the decade, strides were made and members took heart. Although they still had much work to do, Brothers saw that their efforts made a difference. The 1959 camp participants unanimously agreed that the best way to "raise a house average" was to promote an attitude within the house that encouraged study and good grades. They also agreed that involvement in extracurricular activities would build prestige for the chapter on campus, and combining the two and "acting like gentlemen at all times" would result in better relationships with university faculty and administration.

Lending a Hand

Annual regional meetings of alumni further helped strengthen active chapters. Begun in 1947, these yearly meetings resulted in more involved and concerned alumni. In 1950 the meeting specifically addressed academic shortfalls. Alumni arrived at the fourth annual conference bearing written reports from the chapters outlining their problems, and following the Council's directives, the alumni discussed these at length. NIC had starkly illustrated the scope of the problem: thirty-seven out of forty-five DKE chapters fell below the "All Men's Average" for scholarship. Thirteen of those were at or near the bottom on their campuses. To address the problem, the regional chairman formed a committee to survey the situation and report on possible resolutions. Later recommendations included fixing minimum standards for meritorious chapters and addressing public relations problems. The consensus was that rushing chairmen should be serious scholars who would give pledging priority to young men who promised academic excellence.

"...the start a chapter gets can mark its character for good or bad..."

New chapters that did not have alumni were also given support at these meetings because the alumni asserted that "the start a chapter gets can mark its character for good or bad for a prolonged period."

Rewarding Excellence

DKE's earnestness in improving scholarship did not end with committees and brainstorming. While chapter members and alumni struggled to find solutions to the problem, the Council

Sigma Rho's Comeback

Scholarship and good conduct often went hand in hand, and Delta Kappa Epsilon had to deal with her share of unruly offspring. She differed from other fraternities, however, by motivating her chapters to make amends. Sigma Rho's story is but one example of a chapter that faltered and finally triumphed.

The Sigma Rho Deke House in Palo Alto, California, was suspended from the Stanford University campus from spring 1953 to fall 1954 as the result of a drinking party and the chapter's "failure to meaningfully contribute to the university." Though the university permitted members to meet at alumni homes, severe penalties were implemented. Members had to provide their own housing, and no more than three Dekes could live together. The chapter lost rushing and initiation privileges and could not participate in intramural sports. Parties were strictly prohibited. George C.W. Weintz (Sigma Rho, 1955) described how the situation became so bleak in the May 1955 issue of the *Deke Quarterly*:

> Let it suffice to say that there were a few actives who consistently failed to realize that the actions of one or more of them invariably reflected on the entire house. This situation might have been avoided if the house had been more cohesive and better organized. But the returning veterans, tired of regimentation, felt that what one member did was his own concern. The spirit of extreme individualism permeated not only the Deke House but also a number of other fraternities.

The year of suspension gave Sigma Rho members an opportunity to decide whether the chapter would simply die or be revived into an honorable organization with admirable traditions. The Brothers determinedly chose the latter and worked hard to see it happen.

Because of the restrictions placed on the chapter, the members' effort was monumental. Relations within the community needed vast improvement, and obligations with the university needed to be fulfilled. The chapter desperately required organization, and the cost of opening the house again would be prohibitive if new men were not recruited. Against these odds, Sigma Rho rose to the challenge. By the end of the suspension year, members had significantly raised their grades, finishing first in scholastic standing among the twenty-four fraternities for the first time in the chapter's history. And in an effort to establish closer ties with faculty, the Stanford Dekes began a new tradition; each week they invited a professor for dinner and an informal discussion. Because the improvement was so astounding, the university allowed the members to informally rush, resulting in an "outstanding" pledge class of fifteen men. After seeing the determination of the members to reform, the alumni and the Sigma Rho Mothers Club began active involvement in the chapter's success.

Sigma Rho's accomplishment brought resounding praise from the president of the Council, W. Hubert Beal (Delta Pi, 1916). His words appeared in the May 1955 issue of the *Deke Quarterly*.

> The comeback made by Sigma Rho Chapter at Stanford proved that the age of miracles is not past. The Sigma Rho Dekes have richly earned the right to be called a Can-Do Chapter. They have set a shining example which I hope will be a beacon to all Dekes everywhere. In the name of the Council and of our entire membership I salute every Sigma Rho active and alumnus.

developed reward strategies. Through the Deke Foundation, a system of loan programs and scholarship awards was set up to assist worthy students. The foundation was created by the Council in 1951 with Robert Lehman (Phi, 1913), E. Jansen Hunt (Upsilon 1925), and William R. Crawford Jr. (Kappa Epsilon, 1920) as founding trustees. Designed primarily to instill the basic values of the Fraternity among undergraduate Dekes and provide scholarships, the foundation also had the additional purpose of reminding all concerned of the Fraternity's objectives, as outlined in Article II of the DKE Constitution:

A Changing World

In 1948, John Reagan "Tex" McCrary (Phi, 1932) radio, TV and newspaper personality began the long "Draft Ike" campaign for General Eisenhower, who was then president of Columbia University. Tex persuaded Ike to get back into uniform and come to Madison Square Garden to speak to the launch of the new Air Force Association. In 1952, again at the Garden at midnight, after a prize fight, just before the New Hampshire primary, Tex launched the "I Like Ike" campaign. In the Garden, he brought up two special trainloads of young Texans to rally for Ike. Newsreel films of the events were dispatched by air to Eisenhower, then in Paris, to persuade him to run. According to Tex, "Four years later, we used the Garden again for a Rally to persuade President Eisenhower to run for a second term, after his heart attack. Doctors and friends said a second term would kill him; Mamie said: 'It will give him something to live for!' Mamie was right."

Though DKE concentrated on internal issues throughout the 1960s, world affairs did not slip by unnoticed. Fear of Communism, fueled by Sen. Joseph McCarthy's movement to rid the country of "Communists and Fellow-Travelers", gripped the nation in the mid-1950s. Russia's development of the atomic bomb and her unstinted efforts to spread Communism put fear in the hearts of many Americans. At the 112th convention, three young Hungarians, two men and a woman, were DKE's guests of honor. The three had managed to escape from behind the Iron Curtain, and DKE was inspired to commend them for their bravery. The young lady, Katalyn Szigethy, was crowned Convention Queen, and the conventioneers passed a resolution that urged America's fraternities to "lead in aid to and encouragement of their fellow students under the savage Communist yoke in their struggle to gain 'Freedom–the Greatest Fraternity.'"

John Reagan "Tex" McCrary (Phi, 1932) reviews QUARTERLY with Editor Bill Henderson.

"The Objects of Delta Kappa Epsilon are the Cultivation of General Literature and Social Culture, the Advancement and Encouragement of Intellectual Excellence, the Promotion of Honorable Friendship and Useful Citizenship, the Development of a Spirit of Tolerance and Respect for the Rights and Views of Others, the Maintenance of Gentlemanly Dignity, Self-Respect, and Morality in All Circumstances, and the Union of Stout Hearts and Kindred Interests to Secure to Merit its Due Reward."

The Fraternity supplemented the Deke Foundation by establishing the Deke Achievement Awards in late 1955. Hubert Beal, president of DKE, announced the establishment of these awards in the December issue of the Deke Quarterly. The awards would be given yearly to chapters that improved in various areas. Beal explained the Fraternity's incentive to begin a new tradition:

The Deke Awards Program

Each year the International Headquarters of Delta Kappa Epsilon acknowledges the outstanding achievement of undergraduate and alumni members through its awards program. Presentations of awards are made on both the chapter and alumni levels and encompass such areas as excellence in chapter operations, exceptional alumni service, and achievements in personal development and growth. The program consists of ten awards, six for undergraduate performance and four for alumni achievement.

Ken Howe (Phi Gamma, 1994), Bill Norcross (Phi Gamma, 1994), Carmen Davoli (Phi Gamma, 1962) accept Lion Trophy from David Easlick during Banquet 1993. Howe is also the recipient of the DKE Leadership Award, and Davoli also won the Henderson Award.

The **Lion Trophy** is awarded annually to the chapter judged best in overall performance in the previous school year. It is the highest honor that can be achieved by a DKE chapter. Achievement awards collectively represent the four major areas on which the judging of the Lion Trophy is based, but individually they signify the achievement of a chapter in a given area of operation. A bronze plaque is awarded to the chapter ranking first in each of the following areas:

- **Chapter Improvement**–Awarded to the chapter that has exhibited the greatest all-around improvement in such areas as rushing, finances, campus activities, scholarship, community service, and headquarters relations
- **Alumni Relations**–Awarded to the chapter that has done the most to foster improved relations with chapter and area alumni
- **Scholarship**–Awarded to the chapter that has excelled in the development of programs that have improved the chapter's overall scholastic performance
- **Community Service**–Awarded for outstanding creation, development, and execution of one or more public service projects during the year

C. Allen Favrot (Tau Lambda, 1947); his wife, Jane, and Phineas Sprague (Theta, 1950)– Two prior presidents, Henderson Award winners and winners of the Henry H. Michaels, Jr. Alumni Service Award.

The **DKE Leadership Award** is presented annually to the undergraduate who is judged best all-around Deke, based on character, scholarship, and contribution to his school and to Delta Kappa Epsilon.

The **William M. Henderson Alumni Award**, named in honor of DKE's beloved longtime executive director, Bill Henderson (Zeta Zeta, 1939) is a top alumni award presented annually to an alumnus who has given exceptional service to an individual chapter of Delta Kappa Epsilon, not necessarily his own.

The **Henry H. Michaels, Jr. Alumni Service Award**, named in honor of longtime Chairman, "Mike" Michaels (Rho, 1931) is presented periodically to an alumnus who has given great service to the International, as opposed to a chapter.

THE DEKE AWARDS PROGRAM

The **Presidents' Award** is presented in recognition of the personal achievements of an alumnus outside the sphere of Fraternity activities. The award is named in honor of three Dekes who became presidents: Rutherford B. Hayes, Theodore Roosevelt, and Gerald Ford.

The **"Roughrider" Award** is presented to individuals who have fought the "good fight." The plaque contains the T. R. quote "Far better it is to dare mighty things, to win glorious triumphs, even though checkered with failure, than to take rank with those poor spirits who neither enjoy much nor suffer much, because they live in the gray twilight that knows neither victory nor defeat."

The **Honorary President** is elected every two years by the international convention and presides at all public Fraternity functions. He also becomes an ex-officio member of the board of directors. The position is awarded to an alumnus who has exhibited long-standing devotion to the Fraternity and its ideals.

The **Outstanding Alumni Association Award** is presented each year to an outstanding alumni association, and acknowledges excellence of alumni participation in alumni and chapter affairs, not necessarily during any particular period of time.

William M. Henderson Award.

Bill Henderson presenting Henderson Award.

Executive Director David K. Easlick, Jr. (Omicron, 1969) and William Drew Kavan (Theta Upsilon, 1993) present Presidents Award to Senator Russell B. Long (Zeta Zeta, 1939).

Brothers had faced tough issues and worked together for the good of the Fraternity...

> The Council and alumni share the determination of the undergraduates constantly to improve ourselves in scholarship, management of our houses and over-all performance both as individuals and chapters, thus solidly building the strength, stature and prestige of DKE from coast to coast.

The awards would serve other purposes as well. Chapters would find themselves in wholesome competition with one another, while alumni would see their contributions making a difference to DKE.

By the end of the decade, the Fraternity's efforts began to pay off. Not only were DKE chapters more scholarly and cohesive, but in some cases they set examples for other fraternities. Theta Zeta Chapter on the University of California at Berkeley campus was one chapter that went from a small, unmotivated group to one that led by example. Through the undaunting support–and sometimes the unwelcome "interference"–of the alumni, the chapter began to restore "some of the old glitter and strength to the DKE reputation."

Through a carefully crafted plan of improving scholarship and contributing to civic projects, the chapter began to understand its need for an amicable relationship with the university. Scholarship soared, and Theta Zeta's involvement in other activities fostered respect among peers and community members. The chapter's plan became a model for all of DKE as well as the other fraternities on the campus.

The 1950s had been filled with relentless work for the Fraternity, but the efforts were fruitful and timely. As the decade drew to a close, colleges and universities expected a large increase in enrollment as GIs took advantage of education incentives and the first wave of baby-boomers reached college age. DKE faced the choice of enlarging her chapters or encouraging small, solid ones. Either way, overcoming her obstacles had made her stronger and better. Brothers had faced tough issues and worked together for the good of the Fraternity as a whole. She was prepared to meet the challenges ahead.

CHAPTER 8

THE PURSUIT OF EXCELLENCE

When the USSR launched Sputnik in 1957, the United States faced a new reality. While Americans had been disparaging intellectuals and persecuting nonconformists, Soviets had been diligently pursuing technological advances. Suddenly, Americans realized they were falling behind, that strides needed to be made in science and math, and they began asking questions about the nation's educational system. As the 1960s dawned, tension within the United States threatened the country's stability. A large segment of the population no longer trusted the government, and any organization that represented traditional values found itself under siege. DKE was no exception. Though she had fought antifraternity sentiment before, never had the opposition been so loud or effective. Ironically, DKE's survival depended a great deal on clinging to tradition–her tradition of seeking excellence.

STRENGTH FROM WITHIN

Dr. John R. Hubbard (Omega Chi, 1938), dean of Sophie Newcomb College of Tulane University, explained the fears of the country in his 1959 DKE convention address:

> The events of November 7, 1957, made it perfectly clear that Russian science and technology have done wonders. They justify Khrushchev's now famous gesture in this country of the way Russia is closing the gap with the West. And they justify for Americans the most sober

Lieutenant Alan L. Bean (Omega Chi, 1955), Lunar Module Pilot, explains as President Gerald R. Ford (Omicron, 1935) and Astronaut Jack Lousma look on.

reconsideration of their educational programs and a determination to do everything democratically possible to improve them, short of panic.

The public dictum is clear and unequivocal: our institutions must rid themselves of all obstacles to the learning process. For us. . .the significance of the situation is unmistakable. It has become imperative for fraternities to recognize the problems involved with the attainment of intellectual excellence and to be identified with their solution. The alternative is sad to contemplate, for if an appreciable segment of the American public, fearful of survival, becomes convinced that fraternities are a deterrent to the central purpose of education, that membership in a fraternity means that the student will do less academically than he is capable of doing, then college administrators will have no option in the matter of abolishing fraternities.

Hubbard suggested Dekes honestly cultivate a love for learning in themselves and each other, making intellectual potential a major criterion in membership. He recommended encouraging extracurricular activities "of a useful nature" and attracting Merit Scholars to the organization, as well as earning "our share of Phi Beta Kappa and Omega Delta Kappa invitations." If DKE's graduating seniors could be found "in the Rhodes, the Marshall, the Fulbright, the Woodrow Wilson, the

National Science Foundation and a dozen other like competitions," he said, "we shall have demonstrated that membership in Delta Kappa Epsilon is an adventure in excellence."

Yet with the upheaval of the 1960s, fraternities were again under fire, this time because they were seen as allies of "the Establishment." In the May 1961 *Deke Quarterly,* Michael Stramiello Jr. (Mu, 1930), president of DKE, encouraged actives to pursue excellence and urged care in selecting pledges:

> The existence of national and international college fraternities, including Delta Kappa Epsilon, is under criticism by anti-fraternity cults which have sprouted noticeably in recent years. Chapters whose performance is sub par provide effective propaganda material to these cults. Chapters whose accomplishments are above average deprive the would-be saboteurs of the means for carrying out their aim of discrediting fraternities. Strong chapters contribute to the stability of the fraternity and the fraternity system at large. By pledging and initiating only men who have shown promise of creditable achievement in the curriculum, a significant step is taken toward improvement of the chapter and the fraternity.

Dekes took the recommendations to heart and poured more energy into making DKE strong and healthy. Pledge training and initiations became focus areas for improvement, and hazing was curtailed drastically. Scholastic achievement continued to be a priority for all actives as chapter houses instituted quiet hours and study sessions to create an atmosphere conducive to academics. Upperclassmen paired with freshmen pledges in a "scholastic 'Big Brother'" system, and more emphasis was placed on making valuable contributions to the universities and communities. Meanwhile, on the international level, DKE adopted its "Where will DKE be in '73" slogan that reminded the Fraternity to not only address the pressing issues of the day but also to prepare for the future.

Pledge training and initiations became focus for improvement...

Yet the Fraternity's efforts were not enough to stem the negative tide. One member recalled DKE's response to the changing times. "Bill Henderson, who was the executive director at the time, had a lot of fires to put out," he said. "We weren't concerned about historical matters as much as keeping the fraternity alive."

The antiestablishment movement gained momentum as the country became involved in the Vietnam War...

As for DKE's survival, William Dolan (Phi Epsilon, 1955) credits strong alumni organizations that concentrated on strengthening active chapters. "Otherwise, I think we would have lost it in the sixties," he admitted.

Nowhere could that alumni loyalty be better illustrated than through the aid they gave to two chapters that had been devastated by fire. Both Rho and Chi saw their chapter houses burned to the ground in the late-1950s. Immediately after the Rho fire, alumni met with officers of the DKE House Association, insurance adjusters, and college officials to determine what to do next. The college made arrangements to keep the actives together as a group at least part of the time. The College Inn set aside a dining room for the Brothers, and the college alumni association room was made available for meetings. Otherwise, the brothers were scattered, some living in dormitories, others in apartments. The following school year the college supplied the chapter with a small house. For a year and a half the members lived in the temporary facility. Meanwhile the alumni worked to find a new location and to secure funds for the house. When all was told, a beautiful, $250,000 house became Rho's new home, appointed with $5,000 worth of furniture.

Chi's new home was not as elaborate as Rho's, but it could house fifty-six students with adequate kitchen and dining facilities for all, and it cost less than $100,000. Money, time, and expertise were among the gratefully received donations.

Standing Strong, Standing Proud

The antiestablishment movement gained momentum as the country became involved in the Vietnam War and the United States backed its policy of helping any nation threatened by Communism. The 1964 riots at the University of California at Berkeley starkly illustrated the trepidation that gripped the country. More than twenty-eight-thousand students attended that university, and the commotion brought by activists overwhelmed the otherwise quiet community. Theta Zeta Dekes publicly admonished those who had caused the trouble, labeling them a "lost sect" of "disillusioned freshmen and misguided liberals" who had been "raising hell about anything and everything for years."

Dekes in the Spotlight

Ironically, amidst all the criticism of fraternity life, Dekes were among the top achievers of the 1960s. Of note were Dekes in the space program. Lieutenant Alan L. Bean (Omega Chi, 1955) and the rest of the *Apollo Twelve* crew reached the moon on November 19, 1969, taking with them a DKE flag. Four years later, Bean again made the news by commanding a three-man *Skylab Two* crew for a fifty-nine day mission. The purpose was to determine the feasibility of living and working in space for long periods of time. The astronauts also conducted a variety of solar astronomy, earth-resource surveying, and physiological studies.

DKE Flag that went to the moon.

Bean was not the only Deke involved in NASA, however. He was sent on his first moon mission by Dr. Thomas O. Paine (Upsilon, 1942). Paine was appointed administrator for NASA by President Richard Nixon on March 5, 1969. A few weeks later, on March 20, he was confirmed by the Senate and sworn in on April 3, 1969. Paine joined the agency in February 1968 as deputy administrator and became acting head after the resignation of James E. Webb. He told President Nixon, "With your help, Mr. President, I hope to see that the NASA program in the second decade of space exploration will really outperform the accomplishments of the first decade."

A. Bartlett Giamatti (Phi, 1960) and Benno C. Schmidt, Jr. (Phi, 1963)–Two Presidents of Yale.

Amid the excitement of space exploration, Dekes were making impressions in other professions. Perry Lentz (Lambda, 1964) was named Deke of the Year in 1964, the same year his Civil War novel, *The Falling Hills*, took the country by storm.

Tom Landry (Omega Chi, 1946) was another nationally known Deke. The first coach of the Dallas Cowboys, he was named Elder Statesman of the National Football League of Coaches in 1971. During Landry's first nine years with the Cowboys, he turned the expansion team into one of the NFL's powerhouses. Landry went on to enjoy a twenty-eight-year career as the head coach of the team, twice winning the Superbowl championship.

...chapter members worked ever harder to prove their loyalty and contribution to the university...

Though these social activists had been regarded as foolish youths for many years, they began gaining support, and two years before the riots Theta Zeta began to feel the heat. The chapter wrote the following in a letter to the *Deke Quarterly* in 1965:

> Fraternities were labeled hotbeds of religious and racial discrimination, descriptions of "hazing" were given which would have put Himmler to shame, and fraternity men were branded "anti-intellectuals," "throwbacks," and "infantile regressives." We regarded this as a joke at first, realizing that all fraternities are exclusive to some degree. We didn't laugh when the movement resulted in our being forced to sign, on penalty of virtual expulsion from campus, an anti-discrimination pledge forced on us by the university which had bowed to outside pressure. We regarded the pledge as an insult to our integrity in much the same way as we regard our association, as Cal students, with last fall's riots.

Most of the students on that campus were reasonable men and women, and the movement's influence on university policy was a shock. Theta Zeta Brothers admitted where they had gone wrong: "Our great mistake lies in the fact that we have not been as openly dedicated to our way of life as these agitators have been to theirs." The chapter members worked ever harder to prove their loyalty and contribution to the university, drastically improving their academic standing and dedicating themselves to community service.

And they openly supported the troops in Vietnam. By 1966 most Theta Zeta Brothers who had graduated within the previous four years were serving in the Armed Forces. Dekes at Berkeley were no anomaly, though. The war took the lives of fifteen Dekes from twelve chapters. Fraternity members throughout the nation stood behind their country, and the military began to see the positive qualities that fraternities fostered. In recognizing the need for the type of leadership developed in fraternity men, the military made a concerted effort to interest fraternity members across the country in the advantages and opportunities of serving as officers.

A New Direction

The antifraternity movement persisted as the 1970s dawned, yet DKE was determined to outlast it. The continual persecution backfired when it increased the bonds between Brothers in the face of adversity. Perhaps it was this camaraderie that attracted renewed interest in DKE. While many fraternities faltered under the more relaxed attitudes of students, Dekes worked harder to make rush seasons more productive. They were determined not to meet the same fate befalling other Greek letter societies on campus. In a chapter letter to the *Deke Quarterly,* Joe Tegreene (Lambda, 1975) described what he saw at Kenyon in the early 1970s:

> The fraternity is no longer the center of campus activity as it once was. Freshmen no longer pledge fraternities in droves as once was the case. These external forces have, in turn, caused significant changes within the internal structures of the fraternities themselves. Much of the enthusiasm and vigor surrounding. . .fraternity[ies] appears to have disappeared. It is the combination of these internal and external forces that has caused the rapid decline of the college fraternity in the past few years.

Yet Lambda addressed the issues effectively in 1972 by adopting a balanced rush strategy that introduced pledges to all aspects of fraternity life. Large parties were countered by small, intimate get-togethers. Watching football on television was a Fraternity activity, as were occasional games of their own. "Balance was the key–the social as well as the personal, the cooperative as well as the competitive," Tegreene explained. The result was the largest pledge class in the history of Kenyon College. Of the seventy-one freshmen who pledged fraternities that season, twenty-five opted for DKE.

Other chapters faired well, too, and DKE continued to grow. By 1976 seven chapters had joined the Fraternity: Tau Delta at the University of the South, Psi Delta at Wake Forest University, Sigma Alpha at the Virginia Polytechnic Institute, Phi Delta at the University of Western Ontario, Sigma Phi at Villanova University, and Phi Beta at Troy State University.

The growth was a welcome sign of the Fraternity's health, but it also brought to light some sorely needed adjustments. The DKE Council had grown to a cumbersome number of forty-four chapter representatives, many of whom seldom attended meetings, and the Constitution was becoming increasingly outdated.

The growth was a welcome sign of the Fraternity's health...

Rarely can an organization count on a "knight in shining armor" to save the day, but that is what DKE got in Charles O. Blaisdell (Pi, 1937). He was elected DKE President in 1971, and, with the Fraternity in fiscal straits, the attorney and former FBI agent promptly moved the international headquarters out of the expensive Yale Club and into a suite of smaller offices in New

DKE President Charles O. Blaisdell (Pi, 1937) presiding at DKE Council Meeting.

York City where it remained until 1988. Blaisdell, who held the position of president until 1976, (the title was later changed to Chairman of the Board), managed to solve many of DKE's problems by revising the Constitution.

Some of the biggest changes the Fraternity faced centered on its alumni and governing policies. At its 126th Convention, the Fraternity proposed phasing out the DKE Council and replacing it with a Board of Directors as a governing body consisting of a limited number of members and the president of DKE.

Conventioneers approved the changes to the DKE Constitution that included charging a standard initiation fee of fifty dollars and authorizing the president of the Fraternity to allocate a percentage of the fee to new chapters' building funds.

Under Brother Blaisdell's leadership, the Council was reorganized in 1972, becoming an advisory body, and turned the government of DKE over to a new twelve-man working board of directors with one undergraduate member to be chosen at each Convention. Charles H. Lloyd of the newly chartered Sigma Alpha,) was the first to serve in this capacity.

In 1977 the board of DKE's International Headquarters clarified the Fraternity's purpose in a statement of policy that served as a guiding hand for the changing times. Members were reminded that the primary reason for the existence of Delta Kappa Epsilon was to enrich the lives of its undergraduate members and that the focus and direction of planning should be on upgrading those chapters. Then-board member Fred Baxter (Rho Delta, 1939) a Board Member and future Chairman, the major architect of the policy, explained DKE's goals in the Fall 1977 *Deke Quarterly*:

> The Board believes that the primary reason for the existence of Delta Kappa Epsilon is to enrich the lives of its undergraduate members, and that the focus of the Board's planning should be the upgrading of our active chapters.... Our goal is nothing less than excellent accomplishment of ash of the objects [of DKE] by each of our chapters.

The board insisted that to assure the survival of active chapters members must maintain a continuing interest in the Fraternity after graduation. Though this was not a new idea, it was of utmost importance, and the board assumed the responsibility of leading, motivating, and guiding alumni, both individually and in groups.

The Third Deke President

DKE's new direction coincided with the country's impending change of command. The Brotherhood closely monitored Richard Nixon's impeachment hearings and subsequent resignation, which put another Deke in the nation's highest office when Vice President Gerald R. Ford (Omicron, 1935) became the United States' thirty-eighth President. In the Summer 1985 issue of the *Deke Quarterly,* George A. Nicholson Jr. (Omicron, 1928) observed: "None of us knew at the time the role Jerry Ford would play in preserving this nation. His course of reconciliation was the keystone of his short presidency. Reconciliation, as practiced by Ford, was invaluable in preserving the United States of America." *Time* magazine recognized Ford for his honor and cooperative spirit. "In Congress, [where he had served as House Minority Leader] Ford is respected by Republicans and Democrats as not only a clever infighter but also as one who prefers reaching a consensus to twisting arms."

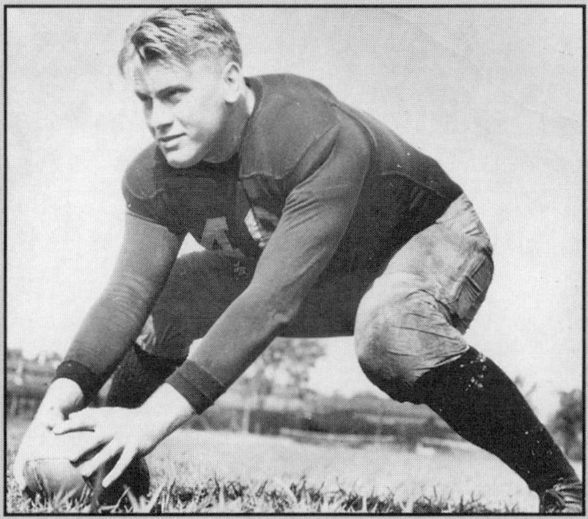

Brother Gerald R. Ford (Omicron, 1935) as a member of the University of Michigan football team.

As a member of Michigan's undefeated national championship football teams in 1932 and 1933, Ford turned down professional football offers from the Detroit Lions and the Green Bay Packers, opting instead to attend Yale Law School.

He was assigned to the House Appropriations Committee in 1951, where he was a member of subcommittees on Foreign Operations, the Department of Defense, and the Army Panel, and he also was appointed to the Select Committee on Aeronautics and Space Exploration. He remained a member of both the Defense and Foreign Operations Subcommittees of the Appropriations Committee and was senior Republican on the Defense Subcommittee before becoming minority leader.

John R. Hubbard (Omega Chi, 1938) with President Gerald R. Ford (Omicron, 1935).

Brother Gerald R. Ford (Omicron, 1935) receiving 80th birthday gift of autographed picture of Brother Theodore Roosevelt (Alpha, 1881) from Executive Director David K. Easlick, Jr. (Omicron, 1969).

Fred A. Baxter (Rho Delta, 1939) and Henry H. "Mike" Michaels, Jr. (Rho, 1931) share a moment at the DKE Club of New York.

We will accomplish this by insisting on acceptable performance where we now are, reviving inactive chapters, and expanding selectively to other campuses where the fraternity system is healthy and strong. We will do this where we feel we can get the best results from the investment of time, money and effort.

Finally, twenty years of struggle drew to a close. Through continual attacks on her very reason for being, DKE had grown in spirit and in numbers. She had answered her critics in the best way she knew: by striving for nothing less than excellence.

CHAPTER 9

AN UNCOMPROMISING STANDARD

In the early 1980s, the pendulum of American ideals began to sway to the right once again. College students developed a renewed sense of values and appreciation for tradition as the country finally recovered from the chaos of the sixties. Fraternities in general began to thrive once more, and by 1981 there were 62 generally recognized male fraternities with 5,500 chapters at approximately 650 institutions of higher learning in the United States and Canada. Total living membership exceeded three million, and chapter houses all over the continent were filled to capacity. *Baird's Manual of American College Fraternities* reported the following message of pride:

> The American college fraternity is an American institution and the chapter in the form it ideally exists on the college campus is a miniature of the larger American democracy. It incorporates mutual selection, congeniality, and common purpose. In assuming his share of work in the group, a fraternity man develops a sense of responsibility for the well being of something outside himself. He learns the great lesson of subordinating self and selfish desires for the good of others. He thus learns to lend his strength to those who have less, thus fulfilling a paramount educational goal.

More Dekes in the White House

The Fraternity's growth in the profitable 1980s filled members with pride, and that grew ever stronger when in November 1988 the people of the United States elected George Herbert Walker Bush (Phi, 1948) to the nation's highest office. Dekes would have been happy enough with that, but President Bush had chosen J. Danforth "Dan" Quayle (Psi Phi, 1969), a Deke legacy, as his running mate. It was only fitting that "The Phi Marching Song" was played at the inaugural parade.

In the Summer 1989 issue of the *Deke Quarterly*, the Editor wrote: "The *Deke Quarterly* has reported a number of significant stories since 1883, but few could have been as deeply satisfying as the presence today of not one but two Dekes in the White House." Indeed, it was the first time in history that the President and Vice President of the United States have been members of the same fraternity.

Vice President George H. W. Bush (Phi, 1948) at 25th Anniversary of President Kennedy's Peace Corps Announcement at the University of Michigan.

Brother George H. W. Bush (Phi, 1948), Thomas Hearn, Jr., President Wake Forest University, Brother Michael Smith (Psi Delta, 1989) and Beth Dawson at Bush/Dukakis debate.

Ever Stronger, Growing Wiser

"A Decade of DKE" became the Brotherhood's new motto, and the standing philosophy was one of continual self-examination. Delta Kappa Epsilon had weathered a disastrous era, and she had not compromised herself in the process. Striving for excellence became a diligent response to the general unrest of the sixties and the prevalent self-indulgence of the seventies. The

More Dekes in the White House

Without knowing it, Bush and Quayle influenced Bill Kavan's (Theta Upsilon, 1992) decision to join DKE. "I thought this was a pretty good example of leadership," he said.

Mike Smith (Psi Delta, 1989) probably has fond memories of that period as well. The political science major set up the first presidential debate held on a university campus, between George Bush and Michael Dukakis. Smith, who had helped coordinate a lecture on Wake Forest's campus by New York Governor Mario Cuomo, approached school officials and suggested that Wake Forest University host a presidential debate. The idea was well received and after much work came to fruition. "This was a student initiated, student involved process from day one," Smith said. The debate was held on September 25, 1988, with fourteen hundred people attending.

Two Dekes run for office.

President Bush accepts Yale University DKE Hat from Winston Bao Lord (Phi, 1990).

On Persistence and Endurance

Sigma Chapter at Amherst College in Amherst, Massachusetts, was originally founded in 1846 as the third fraternity on campus. The chapter thrived for more than 130 years, but toward the end of the 1970s the school encouraged fraternities to admit women, and Sigma acquiesced. The International Fraternity did not condone this violation of the DKE Constitution, which states that membership is open only to male undergraduates, and withdrew Sigma's charter in 1980. During that time, several campus fraternities had chosen to go local. Cutting off the societies from their national organizations was one way the college administrators hoped to rid the campus of Greek letter societies.

The attempt met with failure. Fraternities pursued their activities off campus, and the school administrators decided that they could not tell students what to do off of school grounds. In the mid-1980s male members who had kept DKE traditions alive as "Delta Kappa Sigma" wanted to rejoin DKE. After the Fraternity determined that DKS had "no desire to initiate women" or to otherwise depart from the tenets of the DKE Constitution, the process of establishing a chapter began. The charter was granted in December, 1985, and the initiation ceremony was held February 1, 1986. By summer Sigma had nineteen men.

Brotherhood had survived the siege, learning some important lessons along the way. Attacks on her honor could happen at any time and from any front, and the best way for her to fight them was by adhering to the values established so long ago by fifteen young men who started much more than a club.

The 1980s brought renewed vigor to the Brotherhood, and growth and revitalization followed at its heels. Members realized DKE had not been expanding adequately and a new plan of growth was established in 1984 by concerned Dekes who met in Chicago to discuss ways to strengthen the Fraternity.

The conference suggestions reinforced the growth International sought, and new chapters sprang up. A group of young men at Duke University in Durham, North Carolina, received a DKE charter on April 17, 1983. The chapter chose the designation Epsilon Rho as the initials "ER" matched Duke's official motto, *Eruditio et religio.*

A week later Nu Zeta at Pace University in New York was installed. The group was previously a local fraternity, Sigma Zeta Chi, founded in 1966. In the fall of 1982, the group sought affiliation with Delta Kappa Epsilon and was enthusiastically adopted by the alumni of Nu Chapter, which had gone inactive. Originally, the chapter wanted to call itself Sigma Zeta as an echo of its former name, but finally chose Nu Zeta in appreciation of the Nu alumni.

The growth spurt did not ebb, and Alpha Omega Chapter was installed on May 19, 1984 on the campus of Louisiana Tech University in Ruston, Louisiana. One year later, on April 13, 1985, Theta Upsilon at Arizona State University became DKE's first Southwestern chapter.

Reinstating lost chapters was another priority on which the Brotherhood worked diligently. The efforts met success, and all of "Dekedom" rejoiced when Alpha Alpha at Middlebury was revived in 1985, and Sigma, at Amherst, in 1986. Four more chapters were revived in 1989, the largest single-year addition to the Fraternity since 1856. They were Delta Delta in Chicago, Kappa in Miami, Tau at Hamilton, and Phi Delta at Western Ontario.

Chapters that had long been silent continued to emerge. One hundred years after she had gone inactive, Zeta Chapter was revived at Princeton in 1987. Throughout the university's history, antifraternity sentiment ran high, and by 1882, all of

Rampant Lion Foundation

Founded in 1982 by David K. Easlick, Jr. (Omicron, 1969), the Rampant Lion Foundation was one of the Fraternity's new services. It became DKE's public charity, able to grant chapter loans and individual scholarships while also supporting the Fraternity's "educational mission through tax deductible contributions." The Deke Foundation had not kept up with the changing tax law and was unable to offer to donors the full range of deductibility. It was determined to merge the Deke Foundation into the Rampant Lion Foundation at the earliest possible date. This was accomplished in 1988.

Under the leadership of Honorary Chairmen, Gerald Ford and William E. Simon, the Foundation underwrites educational conferences, historical research and educational materials of the Delta Kappa Epsilon Fraternity.

Union League Club 1985 (left to right) Duncan Andrews, Executive Director, DKE; David K. Easlick, Jr., President, Rampant Lion Foundation; Henry H. Michaels, Jr., Chairman, DKE; James D. Bishop, Vice Chairman, DKE; Robert T. Johnson, Treasurer, DKE.

William E. Simon (Rho, 1952), Former Secretary of the Treasury, pictured here with President Nixon, and serves as Honorary Co-chairman of the Rampant Lion Foundation.

Henry H. "Mike" Michaels, Jr. (Rho, 1931), Chairman, DKE and David K. Easlick, Jr. (Omicron, 1969), President Rampant Lion Foundation, present Vice President J. Danforth Quayle (Psi Phi, 1969) with the DKE PRESIDENT'S AWARD.

The revitalization continued into the nineties as student interest...hit an all-time high...

Princeton's fourteen fraternities were gone. Yet as in days of yore, the desire of students to associate with groups of their own choosing prevailed, and Greek letter organizations reemerged in 1986. Through vigorous efforts by Princeton sophomore Robert Knapp (Zeta, 1988) and DKE Board Chairman Henry H. "Mike" Michaels (Rho, 1931), DKE was among them. A group was formed and on November 6, 1987, Zeta was officially reopened at Princeton as a chapter of DKE.

Omega Chi chapter was also revived; the chapter began in 1900, when an academic and social organization called Capital Club was started at the University of Texas. It became DKE's Omega Chi Chapter in 1913. After more than fifty years, the chapter succumbed to the antifraternity sentiment of the sixties and became inactive in 1971. It was reactivated in 1976

The revitalization continued into the nineties as student interest in fraternities hit an all-time high, in spite of increasing opposition. Beta Chi at Case Western Reserve and Rho Lambda at Oklahoma were reactivated in 1990. Iota Mu at Fordham and Alpha Rho at Temple became chapters in 1991. DKE has added many chapters since then, including Zeta Upsilon at the University of California at Davis, Phi Sigma at Bryant College, Phi Rho at Penn State University, Chi Rho at Bloomsburg University, and Zeta Chi at Bentley College. Phi Gamma at Syracuse and Alpha at Harvard were also reactivated. Kappa Epsilon, dormant for nearly three decades, rejoined the Mystic Circle rejoined the Mystic Circle in 1992. In 1993 Sigma Beta was installed at the University of California at Santa Barbara; Beta Gamma was chartered at New York University; and Omega Omega was chartered at the University of Arizona. In addition, Psi Omega was reactivated at Rensselaer Polytechnic Institute, Troy, New York. The addition of Beta Delta at the University of Georgia in 1995, and the reinstatement of Phi Chi at Rutgers University in 1997, completes the current chapter roll.

BIGGER, BETTER

Such a resurgence was great news for DKE, and by 1991 *Baird's Manual of American College Fraternities,* Twentieth Edition, reported that DKE had fifty-four active chapters, twenty-seven inactive chapters, and a total living membership of forty-thousand. Such growth required some changes to the Brotherhood. The establishing of the Board of Directors was a step in the right direction, but many members believed they were not getting adequate representation with all the directors located

A Time-honored Tradition

On February 4, 1991, South Avenue Deke House at Cornell was officially listed in the National Register of Historic Places and is now part of the National Park Service and the U.S. Department of the Interior. This distinction for Delta Chi Chapter was in recognition of the structure's outstanding American Romanesque Revival style and signified Delta Kappa Epsilon as an important part of Cornell University. Delta Chi secured the property from Cornell University on October 1, 1893, with a one-hundred-year leasehold. On June 20, 1899, Brother Theodore Roosevelt, Alpha '80, was on hand to plant a small Norway spruce. The spruce, pictured next to Roosevelt's left knee, is still there nearly 100 years later.

The tree today.

in New York City, even though it contained the largest concentration of Dekes on the continent. Active and alumni chapters were yearning for board members who were in closer contact and understood their individual needs. Through much debate and hard work, in a December 1984 resolution, the 140th DKE Convention divided the undergraduate chapters into seven geographical regions and restructured the International Board of Directors. The new board consisted of regional representatives elected within each region, and seven Directors at Large, which are elected by all alumni and undergraduate members "in good standing." The fifteenth board member was an undergraduate elected each year by the active members. The board members then elected a chairman, vice-chairman, and treasurer.

Four Presidents of DKE, Duncan Andrews (Rho, 1957), Robert T. Johnson (Zeta Zeta, 1957), Michael Stramiello (Mu, 1930), and Fred A. Baxter (Rho Delta, 1939) at the DKE Club of New York.

For much of the next decade, Delta Kappa Epsilon would be led by Chairman Henry H. Michaels, Jr. (Rho, 1931) Mike, was named Honorary President in 1978, received the Henderson Award in 1980 and was elected Chairman in 1984 (no other man has done all three). Mike, whose two sons became Rho Dekes, is famous for his Lion Marches, and for preserving the DKE Secret Grip which, but for his efforts over the decades, would be more secret than it is–perhaps totally so. An officer of another fraternity once said, "If DKE didn't already have Mike Micheals, they'd have to invent him"; and, of course, he was right. Since 1995, Mike has taken the title, Chairman Emeritus.

A Question of Brotherhood

As DKE addressed issues of growth and success, trouble was brewing on other fronts. Much of it, started in the late 1960s and early 1970s, had never been resolved and was left to fester. When several of the Ivy League schools began admitting women in the late 1960s, fraternities began to pay a heavy price. Under the guise of equal opportunity, some universities and colleges began taking over fraternity houses and making them coeducational. Williams College was one of these, effectively banning fraternities in 1968. Sixteen years later, Amherst and Colby colleges did the same. The argument centered on allowing women into fraternities, but as time went on, the demands continued to mount. DKE has always been adamantly opposed to allowing women into the Brotherhood. With pressures growing at Trinity, Bowdoin, and Amherst, Dekes heatedly debated the issue at the 1980 convention in New Orleans. Some members, in an attempt to keep their chapters alive, were willing to initiate women, but the majority of Dekes stood firm: no women would be initiated into the secret society, and any chapter found doing so would have its charter revoked.

The Board followed up on the resolution of the 1980 Convention, and examined the situation at the various schools where forced coedification was being made an issue by college administrators. From this came the "Bowdoin" solution. The Board of Directors decided that, where required by an overzealous administration, DKE would permit women to be housed in the chapter house, provided that the women were not initiated into Delta Kappa Epsilon. Under no circumstances would a local affiliation entitle one to join the International Fraternity. Attempted violation of this policy resulted in the short term exit of Sigma. The policy was looked at and affirmed at the Toronto Convention in 1982, the San Francisco Convention of 1984, and the Austin Convention in 1986. The issue was hotly debated in Detroit in 1988. Increasingly administrations were becoming more and more radicalized, and more insistent on destroying the Greek system. Deadlines were being set for Northeastern private colleges to rid themselves of single gender organizations.

146th Convention, Boston Banquet at J.F.K. Library.

Just as the heat was reaching scalding proportions, a firm hand was brought to bear on the helm of DKE.

Just as the heat was reaching scalding proportions, a firm hand was brought to bear on the helm of DKE. In 1990 David Easlick, an attorney, and past recipient of the Fraternity's Wm. M. Henderson Award, became Executive Director of the Fraternity. Easlick–whose initials just happen to be D.K.E.–had been involved with International for a number of years. He served on the board of The Omicron Literary Association and was founder of the Rampant Lion Foundation. His list of credits and accomplishments are noteworthy and his efforts as DKE's top professional have been greatly augmented by the support and assistance of his wife, Susan Easlick, the Fraternity's Administrative Director. Under their firm and focused leadership, the Brotherhood has spearheaded the movement to assert the rights of fraternities throughout the nation. "The Easlicks have done so much to bring the spirit of DKE back," said William Simon (Rho, 1952). "I want them to stay as active as they can because we need them."

With the help of the Easlicks, DKE stood firm in the face of increased demands from the admitted "radicals of the sixties" who had stepped into key administrative positions at colleges and universities. Institutions, particularly in the Northeast, became increasingly hostile to fraternities. In *Academic Questions,* David Easlick and Thomas Short, executive editor of that publication, cited examples in their article "Frat Boys at Bay." Middlebury, they said, was one college that required fraternities to either totally reorganize or disband. The reorganization plan stipulated that fraternities must allow women, disassociate with their national organization, drop their Greek-letter names and no longer call themselves fraternities.

The authors noted that pressure to admit women to fraternities spread throughout the nation. Trinity College and Wesleyan University in Connecticut and Pomona College in California forced fraternities to admit women. If the national organizations protested, chapters were ordered to abolish any connection. Likewise, Bucknell College and Colgate University insisted that Greek-letter societies admit every student seeking membership, regardless of gender.

Dekes addressed the problem at a Summer Educational Conference in 1989. They understood that many fraternities, either fearful of losing chapters or forced to change with the times, allowed women to join as members, and in their conference discussions the Brothers meticulously examined all sides of the issue. Yet their decision was no different from any that DKE had reached before: admitting women into the secrets of the Brotherhood was simply unacceptable. At the Boston Convention in 1990, the decision was reaffirmed, and Alpha Chi, Trinity, left the Chapter roll. In 1990 and 1991 the administrations at Middlebury and Bowdoin took the stand that mere membership in fraternities was grounds for disciplinary action. The Fraternity brought suit at Middlebury to defend the free speech rights of our Alpha Alpha Chapter. Although the suit, brought under Vermont State Law, was ultimately unsuccessful, Middlebury, like the Alamo, has become the rallying cry for the Greek System.

148th Convention, New Orleans–Banquet at Antoine's. (From left to right) G. Brent Tynan (Phi Alpha, 1976), Joseph W. DeBragga (Mu, 1943), Robert T. Johnson (Zeta Zeta, 1957), Pat Johnson and (standing) Geoffrey D. Nordloh (Zeta, 1992).

At the 148th Convention in New Orleans a new award was unveiled, named after Theodore Roosevelt's military unit, the "Roughrider" Award. The first three recipients were undergraduates from Alpha Alpha Middlebury, Theta Bowdoin, and Xi Colby. Chris Mastrangelo, Xi Colby 1992, who could have been expelled from Colby had the faculty learned of his DKE affiliation, was elected president of the New Orleans Convention. DKE's stand was trumpeted forth for all to know. Congressman Bob Livingston's (Tau Lambda, 1966) banquet speech on the eventual triumph of free speech over the forces of "political correctness" received 33 standing ovations.

As DKE prepared to celebrate her 150th year, she knew she had come full circle. When she started, her members were shunned by university faculty who regarded them as troublemakers and threats. Now, halfway through her second century, she was experiencing more of the same. Yet this time, she was strong and able to fight back, instead of going underground. This time there were lawsuits, and dedicated alumni and staff who would stand up for the rights of young men to chose their associations. The Fraternity took the lead for the entire Greek System. It incorporated Restore Our Associational Rights, Inc. (R.O.A.R.) with Honorary Chairmen, William E. Simon and former Vice President Dan Quayle. This became the model for the all-Greek Coalition For Freedom of Association. As we go to press, DKE Congressman, Robert L. Livingston, (Tau Lambda, 1966) has introduced a bill in the Congress–The Freedom of Speech and

Christopher Mastrangelo (Xi, 1992) speaking at the Shant Educational Conference.

Association on Campus Act, which will deny Federal funding to colleges that restrict speech and membership in mainline organizations such as fraternities and sororities.

Delta Kappa Epsilon celebrated 150 years of Brotherhood in 1994, and in true DKE fashion, regardless of the tough challenges she faced, a giant party was held in New Orleans, Louisiana, in November 1994 to celebrate. Known as "SesquiGras" the occasion was a week long opportunity to share a wonderful time in New Orleans. Some 500 Dekes and their ladies gathered from throughout the United States and Canada to renew old friendships and revel in Dekedom. (More than 40 had not had enough at the end of the week and continued on to Natchez and Vicksburg for more excitement!)

SesquiGras proved to be an excellent opportunity to sound out alumni opinions of the Fraternity: "When I graduated, every Deke I knew was successful," said William Dolan (Phi Epsilon 1955). "And I don't think it had anything to do with their education."

In addition to the celebrating, the sesquicentennial also held an auction in which Deke-related items, including a football signed by Tom Landry, a beautiful DKE quilt with the rampant lion and DKE heraldry stitched on it, a framed autograph of Dan Quayle, fishing trips to British Columbia, and two framed color sketches of "Mount Dekemore" with the likenesses of DKE's four presidents, were offered to the highest bidder. This "Silent Auction" has become the major annual fund-raiser for the Rampant Lion Foundation.

Chairman James D. Bishop (Phi, 1956), Honorary Co-chairman William E. Simon (Rho, 1952) with George Plimpton at a Rampant Lion Foundation Fundraiser in New York City.

Billy and Francis Treadway (Zeta Zeta).

David Easlick, Bob Johnson, Mike Michaels with Congressman Robert L. Livingston (Tau Lambda, 1966).

Omicron (below): Bill and Polly Larned, Mary Anne Zinn, David Easlick, Dick Kost, Mary and Bill Hurley, Stephanie Kost, Susan Easlick, Bill Krag, George Zinn and Wendy Krag.

Bob Livingston (Tau Lambda), Bill Simon (Rho), Allen Favrot (Tau Lambda), Jim Bishop (Phi), John Wilson (Mu), Jim Makrianes (Sigma), John Stembler (Beta).

Rusty Barkerding (Zeta Zeta) and Charlie Blaisdell (Pi).

John Guyton (Delta Kappa) and Jim Makrianes (Sigma).

DKE invades Vicksburg.

Right: Theta Upsilon–Jeff Krieg, Eric Hartel, Bill Kavan, Martin Hernandez, Sean O'Brian, John McCabe, Paul Giles, Brent Summers, Eric Maul.

Pledge Brothers: C. Allen Favrot and Shep Pleasants, Tau Lambda.

Above: Peter Bianchi (Lambda), Eric Peniston (Delta Chi), Rob Bridges (Lambda).

Left: Jim Makrianes (Sigma), Bill Simon (Rho), John Wilson (Mu) and Bill Dolan (Phi Epsilon).

Top Left: David Elder (Zeta Zeta) recites "Brothers in DKE" as Bill Dodenhoff (Tau Lambda) and Al Bienvenu (Zeta Zeta) hold the candles.

Top Right: Bob and Carole Pettit (Zeta Zeta).

Middle Left: Charlie Blaisdell (Pi) and David Easlick (Omicron) present posthumous Henderson Award for Robert T. Johnson (Zeta Zeta) to Bain and Pat Johnson.

Middle Right: Zeta Zeta—Wilbur Reynaud, Jack Salisbury, Madeline Gill, Al Bienvenu, Bo and Conway Farrell, Betty Bienvenu, Linda Salisbury and Clave Gill.

Bottom Right: David Akridge (Tau Lambda), Ingersoll Jordan, John Seago (Beta), Gordon Smith (Phi Alpha), Susan Seago, Betsy McKean, George McKean (Omicron), John Stembler (Beta).

Top Left: Jean and Doug Laidlaw (Theta Rho), Pamela and Cecil Convey (Tau Alpha).

Middle Right: Psi grouping–Mike Klyce, James Pittman, Walker MacDonald, Mason McGowin and David Stewart.

Bottom Right: David and Susan Easlick at 150th in New Orleans.

The celebration was an example of the pride Dekes take in their Fraternity, a Brotherhood of like minded men who celebrate their common ideals as well as their personal differences. The stipulations specified by the founders of DKE have changed little over the years. "I think our success goes back to what the founding fathers were looking for: we're gentlemen, scholars, and jolly good fellows," commented Doug Laidlaw (Theta Rho, 1943). Charlie Blaisdell (Pi, 1937) summed up everything DKE had stood for in the past century and a half, the purpose for all her triumphs and struggles: "The great emphasis in belonging to Delta Kappa Epsilon is the feeling of a person being your brother by choice and not by chance. DKE is not good because it's old–it's old because it's good."

And so, as the History of the First Century and a half of DKE goes to press, some three years after the event, Delta Kappa Epsilon continues strong and united. We serve under our Chairman, world renowned industrialist and master yachtsman, James D. Bishop (Phi, 1956) whose long service to Phi and to DKE rests on the bedrock principle that never will a chapter of DKE be lost because a strong international organization was not there to help. And Dekes continue to set the standard in all endeavors: in the business world, Herb Kelleher (Gamma Phi, 1953) has set the airline industry on its ear with his highly successful SOUTHWEST AIRLINES, while Frederick Smith (Phi,

1966) dominates the worldwide overnight shipping business in FedEx–the idea for which was Fred's Yale thesis which was scorned by the Yale Prof! And who can walk down a street anywhere without encountering Don Fisher's (Theta Zeta, 1951) amazing success story–The Gap–which grew out of Fisher's complaint that he couldn't find a store that stocked every size in blue jeans. In the military, when NATO decided to put troops into Bosnia, another DKE, ADM Leighton W. "Snuffy" Smith, Jr. (Psi, 1961) was chosen to command all Allied Operations. DKE's hold on politics was displayed to a worldwide audience at the 1996 Republican Convention, as the three prime time speakers, Gerald Ford (Omicron, 1935), George W. Bush (Phi, 1968) and George H.W. Bush (Phi, 1948) headed to the podium. Even the 1996 World Series was a DKE event! Losing Braves Chairman, Bill Bartholomay (Delta Epsilon, 1950), promised revenge on winner George Steinbrenner's (Epsilon, 1952) Yankees.

As we prepare to enter the 21st Century, we are blessed by having President Gerald R. Ford (Omicron, 1935), William E. Simon (Rho, 1953) and Vice President Dan Quayle (Psi Phi, 1969) as Honorary Chairmen of the various DKE entities, with James D. Bishop (Phi, 1956) as the Chairman of DKE, Phineas Sprague (Theta, 1950) Chairman of R.O.A.R., and David K. Easlick, Jr. (Omicron, 1969) President of the Foundation, at the helm. This book is dedicated to them and to all the men who have thus far come into the bonds of brotherhood, and all those who will enter the Mystic Circle in the glorious future.

VIVE LA DKE!

Gerald R. Ford (Omicron, 1935) visits "new" Omicron Chapter House in 1983.

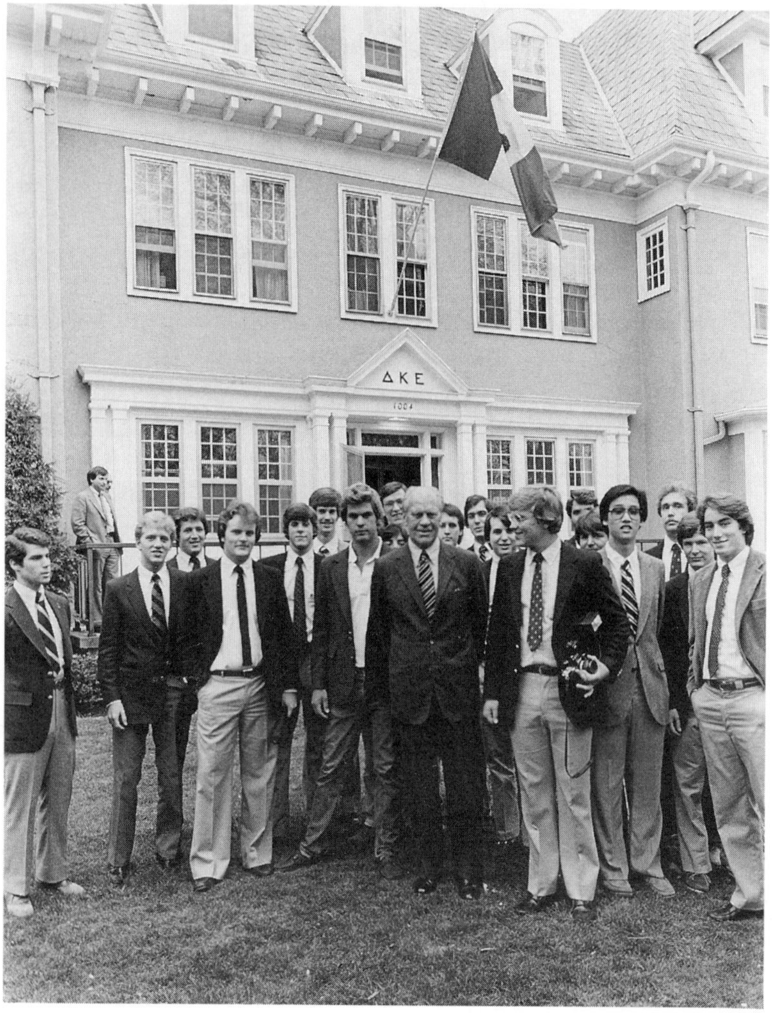